HOW TO INCREASE YOUR MONEY-MAKING POWER

How To Increase Your Money-making Power

BY

JOHN ALAN APPLEMAN

New York

Frederick Fell, Inc., Publishers

TO MY TWO JEANS

Without whose capacity for spending
the knowledge in this book would have
been unnecessary

New, revised edition, 1964

Copyright © MCMLIX by John Alan Appleman

For information address:
Frederick Fell, Inc.
386 Park Avenue South
New York 16, N.Y.

Published simultaneously in Canada by
George J. McLeod, Limited, Toronto

Manufactured in the United States of America

Contents

Publisher's Preface

With pride, we present one of the finest books on money-making ever published!

Here is a small taste of what's inside, in question and answer form, as follows:

QUESTION 1: **There are at least four ways to buy a going business with absolutely no cash, and without borrowing one cent from a bank! Can you name them?**

ANSWER: To begin with, you can give the former owners stock in your own company which is the way most large corporations buy other firms, without one cent of cash changing hands. You can do this with any publicly-owned company, large or small, and with many privately-owned firms as well.

Secondly, there is the option route, with payment of the option money delayed until you can earn it back from a second purchaser. Thus, this second purchaser pays your option dollars for you.

You can pay for the company in future royalties, such royalties to be earned from the sale of the company's products when you take it over. You can guarantee that you will pay a minimum yearly royalty or the company reverts back to its original owners; but this still doesn't commit you for a cent of cash to pick the company up.

There are several other methods of paying the former owners out of future profits. It is suggested that you turn to the chapter on MAKING MONEY BY BUYING IN for a futher discussion.

QUESTION 2: **At what point do smart-money men start selling stocks that are still going up?**

ANSWER: Quite simply, when other stocks are going up even faster. You see, you only have so much money to invest. Even though the stocks you now own are doing well, if other stocks are climbing faster, it may be good policy to switch over to them. Take the big dollar first—the smaller dollars only if you have money (and time) left over. See the chapter on the STOCK MARKET.

QUESTION 3: **Every day, opportunities arise where you can make a life-long annuity without investing a cent, simply by making a phone call! Do you know how to detect and exploit them?**

ANSWER: By becoming a middle-man, getting somebody else

to invest the risk capital, and collecting what may be a sizable royalty for bringing two parties together. For explanation, see page 66.

QUESTION 4: **Where in your daily newspaper—and not in the financial pages—can you find the best source of 100% or better profit deals?**

ANSWER: Believe it or not, in the obituary columns. See chapter 3 for the reasons behind this surprising phenomenon.

QUESTION 5: **Can you name the five Bonus Sources of income you should get from your business deals—where other people pay you to let them make you money!**

ANSWER: These bonuses (that you should always ask for in every deal where they apply) are: 1. Royalties, over and above selling price. 2. Salary, if you are to have any contact with the business at all, even for a few hours a week. 3. Percentage of gross—*not* profit, because this way *you* get paid first, even if the business loses money. 4. First payment from profits if you can't get 3 above where you collect before anyone else. 5. Guaranteed collateral for your money—if you put any up. On fixed assets, etc. This remarkable book will teach you how to protect yourself in any business deal.

QUESTION 6: **Name three tiny mistakes in negotiation that will mark you as a "patsy" to the smart-money man? Do you know how to avoid them?**

ANSWER: To further protect yourself, avoid these "Amateur-Investor Errors". 1. Naivete—ignorance of the field, the market, the particular company you're interested in, the people with whom you're dealing, etc. See chapter 1 for a fuller discussion. 2. The failure to reduce agreements to writing. You can't take anyone's word in a business deal—even if he's completely honest. Remember that there may be misunderstandings or hazy memories which will destroy your advantages. 3. Get all the figures—on overhead, taxes, maintenance, future commitments, etc. See the Real Estate chapters in this book.

QUESTION 7: **There are at least four simple demands that you should make in speculative deals that almost certainly guarantee you a profit! Do you know what they are, and exactly when you should make them?**

ANSWER: Again, *DEMAND*—don't be afraid to ask for— 1. Royalties. 2. Salary. 3. Percentage of Gross. 4. First payment from property. 5. Guaranteed collateral for your money.

Please read this book. Study it. Memorize it. Make its rules of opportunity-exploitation and self-protection second nature.

—THE PUBLISHERS

Introduction

THE ENTHUSIASM with which the first edition of this work was received has been most flattering. Its selection by the Executive Book Club and recommendation by reviewers has made it worthwhile to undertake this revision.

For this edition, I was asked to intensify and expand certain phases of the discussion in which particular interest existed. Particularly this is true of the discussions relating to the stock markets and to real estate investments. In order to expand these, I have deleted certain chapters dealing with the development by the individual of his own abilities and selection of a vocation, since those ordinarily require personal consultation and help by qualified persons—and also certain esoteric aspects of investment which most of us seldom encounter.

I do want to thank those splendid industrialists and financiers who assisted in the first edition of this work and who gave of their accumulated knowledge so generously. I also want to thank those persons who are mentioned in this work and whose success stories helped to inspire others to like efforts. In addition, references in this work to *Operation Success* are to the book by that title, authored by Quentin Reynolds and Wilfrid S. Rowe, 1957, published by Duell, Sloan & Pearce, Inc. The references to Walter Chrysler are taken from his autobiography entitled *Life of an American Workman*, 1950, published by Dodd, Mead and Company. References are made to other helpful treatises and discussions throughout the text.

John Alan Appleman
January 15, 1964

1

Make Yourself Inflation-proof
and Depression-proof

LET'S BEGIN by pointing out a little of what, in the line of human nature, is likely to bring success. Then let's go on to the broad concept of investment, which is just about the best way for anyone to succeed in making money.

As we go along, you'll see that it really is possible to set up safeguards against both depression and inflation. You'll see exactly what happens to your money at these times. We'll discuss, briefly, a number of ways to keep your money growing at a steady rate.

Whatever your choice of career, and whatever your mode of life, you should begin thinking early about letting your money make money for you. This means that, however modest it may be, one should start his investment program early. Of course, in so starting it, he should not be so young that he does not know what he is doing; although, even then, it may be worth many dollars for him to make his mistakes early.

Know what you are investing in

I took a flier at becoming a financier at the age of five. At that time, in 1917, all children were saving their dimes in dime banks to buy Liberty stamps and bonds. It was obvious to me that grown-up people did not realize the value of money. Here they were giving two great big coins, nickels, for one tiny coin, a dime. Seeing the obvious fallacy in what they were doing, I started out to corner the nickel market. By the time I had exhausted my round bank of its supply of dimes, trading the smaller for the larger (I was generous even in those days), some kind person explained to me the difference in metals and I quickly got out of the market—poorer, but wiser.

Even as I learned that there are such things as baser metals, it is important for each individual to learn that there are bad, as well as good, investments. One of the tragedies in life is the fact that frequently people have no surplus to invest until their later years. Then, if they have had no investment experience, an unwise investment may strip them of the funds intended for retirement. Early investment, even if occasionally unwise, may by bitter experience teach one wisdom which he will not gain through reading books, because he may refuse to profit by the mistakes of others.

Shoemaker, stick to your last!

Another area of investment, which is rarely understood as such, is the hidden investment which is made while progressing through life. This hidden investment includes many things which are often not appreciated as being investments—the ownership of one's home, in which the equity steadily increases as the mortgage is paid off; the life insurance which one purchases and gradually pays for; the pension plan which is carried by the corporation; the social security payments which one approaches as he grows older; and the small stock held in the building and loan association or credit union. If these things averaged out, over a thirty-year period, together with other savings or investments, at $1,500 a year (and in peak years they may be considerably greater), the total accumulation alone would amount to $45,-000. Interest earned and enhancing the total—even without rising capital values—would bring this to an amount in excess of $60,000. Therefore, it is clearly not necessary to plunge into risky or untried ventures in an effort to achieve financial security too rapidly. One is more apt to lose his entire capital accumulation by trying to compete in an unfamiliar field.

This book would be well worth the amount of work involved in its creation if the reader remembers only the statements contained in this one paragraph. There is an old saying that "A shoemaker should stick to his last." This is one of the truest statements I know. Every field of human endeavor is highly competitive. When a man successful in one field takes the surplus there acquired and tries to pyramid it into a quick fortune in a field of which he knows nothing, he is a fool. He is betting his savings that he can outwit men of sagacity, resourcefulness, and years of constant experience at their own game, one in which many intelligent people familiar with the field have gone bankrupt. Even if it is not a competitive type of endeavor, one must have the most pristine faith in man to take the judgment and word of another that an investment is sound. That confidence is, at least 90% of the time, misplaced. Each year I see dozens of able business and professional men lose their entire surpluses through discontent at slow accretion and urgency for retirement, yet no dissuasion will stop them. Shoemaker, stick to your last!

By this I do not mean that one should never make an investment. It is only the foolish steward who buries his gold talent in the ground. There is a difference, however, between reckless and sound investment, and there are always sound investments of some character. The investor should study with great care all possible fields of investment and become intimately familiar with their benefits and hazards. He must progress beyond the point where he thinks he knows all about any phase of investment. That is the place of danger. No field of finance is that simple. Then he must begin to talk with real experts in that field, read books and articles upon the subject, and learn the problems and dangers. There is hardly any investment which is absolutely, one-hundred per cent safe, but knowledge can greatly reduce the risks.

College sense is not always common sense

Nor are college-trained men necessarily any wiser investors than those not possessing college degrees. As a matter of fact, lawyers and physicians are notoriously easy marks for the professional confidence man, as well as for the promoter of highly speculative securities. I remember as a boy that the physicians in the community in which I then lived had invested, almost to a man, in gold mine stock. That particular promoter cut a wide swath through the professional ranks. Ten years ago, I noticed that physicians were being taken right down the line upon wildcat oil well speculations. I wondered why professional men constituted particularly easy prey for such persons; then I finally learned the answer. At that time in life, those persons are for the first time earning substantial surpluses, after many lean years of education and special training. Their entire experiences have been in professional matters—not with investments. Therefore, the possession of these surpluses bothers them; they want to invest them wisely, in the hopes of an early retirement; and, having no experience with investments, they are persuaded by the promoter. In such a situation, a wisely planned investment program supervised by competent investment counsel is much sounder. It may grow more slowly, but there is less risk of those surpluses being wholly lost.

It is not possible, of course, to find an investment counselor in any area who is expert upon all possible methods of investment. The stockbroker is no expert upon farms or rental real estate. Nor should the average individual use an attorney or an accountant as his adviser in those respects. They have proper functions to perform within their own fields, but their training does not render them expert in the field of investment, and it is an imposition for the client to demand services of them for which they have no greater training than the client himself.

Ask the man who does the work

If the client were considering buying a tavern, then certainly he should talk to people in the tavern business who know the possibilities and the dangers in that field. If he is considering buying a farm, certainly he should talk to a capable farm manager. No person is omniscient outside of his own field, perhaps not even within it. As we proceed with the discussion of this in the next few chapters, we will try to point out some of the pitfalls as well as the guideposts to be followed, the puddles into which one may slip and fall, as well as the paths which skirt them by.

Recognizing these limitations, there are a few general rules relating to investment which I would like to summarize first, and which we will discuss in greater detail in the appropriate places. Those rules are as follows:

1. One of the peculiar rules of investment is that the best time to invest, as a rule, is when others are following an opposite course. Most people sell stocks, farms, or other property in the middle of a depression. That is the best time, of course, to buy—not on the boom markets when the income, averaged over a twenty-year basis, may not return over 2 per cent annually upon the investment.

2. Try to diversify your holdings to the extent that 25 per cent or better of net worth is in "equity holdings"—such as soundly chosen common stocks. The younger man's holdings of this type may run from 50 per cent to 75 per cent.

3. If you cannot afford a widely diversified stock portfolio, check over investment syndicate stocks or mutual fund shares which offer this diversification. However, study their past records with care and bear in mind that an excellent record for the period from 1940 onward does not mean that a like result would follow if we encountered a new era similar to that from 1929 to 1938. Also, buy for the long pull, and, if a young man, preferably in the field of "growth type" securities. Don't purchase stock research services in an effort to try to become your own expert. Many brokers have read them for years and are far from being financially secure.

4. If you buy farm land, buy it in your own county or near home where you can talk to the tenant over the telephone, watch his performances, and replace him if necessary. Buy the best land, not the poorest, though it costs you more —but buy it in a period when the price is not three times its average cost over the past twenty years. And don't put the money back into farm houses, etc. Such items are nonproductive and expensive. Land with no buildings at all, rented out to an adjacent farmer, is usually the most satisfactory—unless you choose to live on the farm yourself.

5. If you buy rental real estate, don't buy the lovely and expensive properties—for example, a thirty-thousand-dollar property which brings in $150 a month. Buy, instead, property which will gross between fifteen and twenty-five per cent per year, and net not less than ten per cent. It may not give you the pride of possession—but it's a far better type of investment. And commercial real estate, for many reasons, is generally better than residential real estate.

6. The individual must select investments which fit his personality. One person will gravitate naturally toward farms; some will shun rental real estate, because of fear of vacancies, plumbing bills, etc.; some have a phobia of the stock market.

★   *Each person should select the type of investment with which he will be content, but seek to diversify his holdings between dollar type and equity type of holdings so that he can face the hazards of inflation and deflation with equal equanimity.*

7. One who is an investor should bear in mind the possibility of health hazards such as "little strokes" which may affect his business acumen in later years and cause the dissipation of his funds. It would not be amiss, after the investment program is quite well crystallized—perhaps by age 50—to shift the assets to a corporate trustee, with reasonable restrictions against one's own improvidence, as much as can be done consistently with prevailing state law. And if one is fearful of his own judgment, he can use the corporate trustee even before that time, although such trustees normally tend to be ultra conservative in their investments, which normally will not make for growth of the investment.

8. Look out for the unconventional investment. For example, good Canadian securities may become excellent investments because an industrial boom is expected to occur in Canada similar to that which we experienced in the United States long ago. However, many fly-by-night bucket shops are set up in Canada, particularly in Toronto, from which place they send barrages of literature to the suspected sucker in the United States. But they do more than that. They will send out telegrams, or call him upon the telephone about a particular stock, and are expert in the conversations which bring in the dollars. Wherever one receives telegrams or telephone calls about a stock issue, from across the border, he had better close his ears to the siren song and keep his money in his pocket. The same is true of the so-called "penny stocks." These are found particularly in mining ventures, such as uranium and other items where a promoter on the fringes of a territory where uranium, gold, copper, or other mineral, is found sets up a corporation and promotes it at substantial cost, of which expenses he is the principal beneficiary. Avoid the unconventional investment. Once out

of ten times a person may lose by heeding that advice; nine times out of ten, however, he will profit thereby.

Get acquainted with capital gains

In considering any type of investment, it is most important that the investor be familiar with an important concept arising out of our income tax laws. That is the concept of "capital gains."

A simple illustration will show what I mean. Let us take Willie Mays, for example, making a pretty terrific income as a baseball player, and having no tax break by reason of the fact that he is a bachelor (I believe he now is). Let us suppose that Willie buys $100,000 of an unusually good common stock which pays a 10 per cent dividend. Willie is, at the time of this writing, in approximately an 89 per cent tax bracket—unfair, of course, but true. So each dollar of this 10 per cent dividend which Willie receives is tacked onto his already high income; Uncle Sam takes $8,900 of the dividends, and Willie takes $1,100—a return of 1.1 per cent upon his money. If the dividend had been the more normal one of 5 per cent, he would have been left only one half of one per cent on his investment.

Therefore, Willie, like many others, must turn to the concept of capital gains. Under our income tax laws, any investment, not connected with one's own trade or business, if held for six months and then resold, is taxed upon a different basis than earned income. The profit resulting from the sale —the difference between cost of the item purchased and its selling price—may be reported as income and only one half of it would then be taxed. Willie, in that situation, would then pay a 44 per cent rate upon such profits instead of 89 per cent. But, still better, Willie could elect to pay under an optional tax basis and pay 25 per cent of his gain as tax, leaving 75 per cent for Willie—and, if he does bite a lemon now and then, the losses may be deducted from capital gains of a like character. In the case of certain of such investments, such as in oil and gas, a loss resulting from them would be deductible as a business expense, so Willie does not lose much if he wants to take a flier in them.

Incidentally, with reference to items which have increased in value, if Willie should hold those investments in their inflated form at the time of his death, there would be neither income tax nor capital gains tax chargeable to his estate upon the profit. Estate taxes might take a nibble, but they would take the same nibble if Willie had sold those investments shortly before his death and reduced them to cash. The moral is that any person who is making plans, because of advanced age or ill health, to have an early need for estate administration should not sell appreciated assets. Also, if one is going to give a substantial gift to charity, he should give inflated stocks and let the charity sell them, instead of giving cash. The charity derives as much benefit, and the taxpayer saves taxes.

Short-term vs. long-term profit

This principle of capital gains is of the utmost importance. It is the basis of almost every investment growth program. Its principles must be understood. One must always also understand that short-term gains—that is, the profit which is taken when an item is held for less than six months after buying it—is the same as ordinary income. We are definitely talking of longer term investment gains.

The reason why capital accretion is so very important is because of the progressive history of dollar devaluation. If the history of this country were marked off in ten year intervals since 1851, it would show a most alarming change. The chart will look like a series of stair steps. It will move sharply upward, then slightly down, then upward again and so on. The bottom of the downgrade never reaches the bottom of the previous upclimbing line. For example, in 1890 one could build a type and size of house for $3,500 which would now cost $75,000. In proportion, a man who left an estate of $25,000 was then considered well-to-do. It would take ten times that amount now to support a widow and children in the same degree of comfort.

Keep your gold in circulation

What's the result? The man who buries gold worth $1 in the ground, at our present rate of devaluation, winds up with 25 cents in his normal life span, and if the dollar is put out at interest during his 30 years of business activity and triples in value, he still has only 75 cents. This means that the normal individual must do one of two things with dollars—he must make them expand at an abnormal rate from capital gains, in order to catch up with their loss of value; or he must invest them in things which will not only return income, but will inflate in value in proportion to the loss of the dollars. There are other problems which will be pointed out—safety, credit, liquidity, etc.—but this problem, so simply stated, is the basic need of all modern investment programs. All plans must be directed toward meeting those needs or they will fail.

Naturally, investment programs must look to investments both in periods of prosperity and periods of deflation. There are good opportunities in both times. The possibilities of tremendous bargains usually, although certainly not always, arise during the very middle of depressions when dollars are hard to find for such investments. In order to purchase, one must have either money or credit; particularly in times such as described. Therefore, he must avoid overextension, and he must arrange for dollar availability which he can utilize irrespective of bank regulations, credit restrictions, or low market value of his own investments.

Special nests for your nest-egg

If one wants to be assured of available funds in times of depression, there are many ways in which this can be accomplished. In the 1930's some people simply kept cash in their lockboxes. This is not to be recommended. Not only is it unsound, from a point of public or social policy, but it is unwise personally. For one thing, occasionally money disappears from lockboxes. It takes a very clever thief, but it has been done. And I do know of one situation in Chicago where a lady who took certain papers out of the box failed to replace $10,000 in cash when she returned the box to the vault.

It is far wiser to have such things as United States government bonds or other securities which can be cashed under any circumstances without a shrinkage of principal. Some building and loan stocks can be cashed rather quickly, but most of these allow themselves sixty or ninety days, as a minimum, if they desire to enforce such waiting periods when money is short, and they may. For this particular purpose, common stocks are no good, because they depreciate with the rest of the market in times of depression. Preferred stocks of good industries may depreciate somewhat less, but they will still depreciate. So far as bonds are concerned, they have no greater assurance of safety. I remember the general counsel of a prominent corporation telling me 20 years ago that when the 1929 depression hit, he thought he would be smart, so he sold his common stocks and kept his bonds. The common stocks, he said, depreciated grossly, but the bonds were wiped out, and the common stocks later again increased in value. A cousin of mine, then a prominent neurologist in Chicago, had tremendous holdings in mortgage bonds of apartment houses and hotels. He told me that he took an average 50 per cent loss straight across the board on those securities. Therefore, bonds are not necessarily the answer for quick cash in times of depression.

Virtues of high-premium insurance

My own recommendations are very definite. One should always, of course, have a moderate amount of cash on deposit. This is the current expense fund. He should also have a somewhat larger amount in government bonds. This is the secondary reserve, or emergency fund. But, for the larger reserve or possible investment fund retained for depression use, the logical answer is high premium payment life insurance. By that I mean something on the order of twenty-payment life policies with a good company, which furnish a feature of estate accrual and insurance protection while building up reserves fairly quickly. If one initiates such a program early, even five or six years of premium payments upon a respectable policy, permitting dividends to accumulate, will build up a rather fair loan value. Many men will prepay ten years' premiums at inception. If they should die before ten years have expired, the face of the policy plus the unearned premiums go to the beneficiary. If a depression occurs, the loan value is substantial. If it does not, the premuiums are earning interest constantly and in a form where the insured may not have to report their interest earnings, or dividends, as income for tax purposes.

A man whose financial worth in other respects equals $100,000 should have an equivalent amount of life insurance. As another point, a small amount of money may prevent his principal business from collapsing in an emergency—and funds may not be available through any source other than a policy loan. In addition, one possesses a certain peace of mind from having bought an estate upon the installment plan, as he does with life insurance; and banks regard him as a much better credit risk. His sense of responsibility is deemed, and accurately so, to be high.

Bearing in mind the fact that we will later be discussing stock market investments, let us look to some of the other savings or sources of investment of surplus funds which are commonly used, and study the advantages and disadvantages of each. Here are some of them:

1. Government bonds. Government bonds vary widely in rates of interest available, valuation from time to time, and redemption period. Normally, keeping in mind the interest

return, goverment bonds do not make a good investment except for purposes of quick cashability.

To illustrate how much they may vary, some years ago I advised a newly organized life insurance company to sub-scribe for an issue of government bonds, for the purpose of its required state deposits. They purchased $200,000 of such United States government bonds bearing a 4 per cent interest rate, which was then excellent. In fact, it was a better average yield than most life insurance companies could secure from investments across the board, and with no responsibility for supervision. One year later, the same company had a problem of investing additional funds, and we were scratching to find a one and one-half per cent return in shorter term government bonds. Now, of course, interest rates are much higher because of the oversupply of govern-ment bonds. Series E bonds, which are popular with the small investor, over the first ten-year period will return an average of 3.3 per cent, non-compounded, with a very slow rise in the early years in the event one has to cash them.

One way to make a good deal

Occasionally some state bonds can be bought on a favorable basis. One year, I bought some Illinois toll road bonds at 70. This means a discount from their redemption value of almost 30 per cent. Since they pay approximately 3.6 per cent, income-tax free, their real value to me was double that; and, since they were bought at a discounted basis, the practical return was approximately 12 per cent per dollar invested. Of course, such bonds are repayable only out of specific funds; but, in this particular situation, I could be pretty confident that Illinois could not afford to let that issue go into default, since it wanted to sell other bonds of a similar type at a later date.

2. Municipal, or other special assessment, bonds. This de-pends upon several factors. A person must, first, always be sure that the proceedings were valid—and sometimes in-

validity may not appear for several years. However, the opinion of good bonding attorneys approving such issue (and not the opinion of some small town corporation counsel) is usually a sufficient safeguard. Next, one should never buy special assessment bonds which are issued upon improvements in a new subdivision where homes are yet to be built. Many promotions fail, and the value of the improvements may exceed the value of the land. Nor should bonds be purchased in an area which is badly run down or occupied by ramshackle or slum-type housing. Assessment bonds should only be purchased in good business areas or good residential areas, where a default of payment would cloud the title to the property and induce the owner to keep his installments current.

The next factor is the interest rate. Certain types of bonds may bear an interest rate of only about 2 per cent. Others frequently bear 5 per cent and are equally desirable. At the present time, as pointed out with reference to the Illinois toll road bonds, the income from municipal bonds is tax free, although Congress periodically has under consideration legislation to change this.

3. Bank deposits. The yield has improved in recent years upon time banking accounts. It certainly is not necessary to carry all of one's funds in a checking account, when a savings account does pay reasonable interest. In the case of emergency funds such as we have been discussing, in addition to those amounts required for commercial use, a savings account is a logical answer.

4. Savings and loan, or building and loan, associations. This depends wholly upon the managements and method of administration. Dividends ordinarily run now between 4 and $4\frac{1}{2}$ per cent. If the management is sound, its loans are diversified and made upon a conservative basis, there is no no better interest type investment of money for purely modest interest yields. Even if some properties have to be foreclosed in a depression period, these would be fractional, and the property thus acquired at not to exceed 65 per cent of

the value assigned for loan purposes would ordinarily be sound in the portfolio. But if a company makes loans upon fraternity or sorority buildings, fraternal lodges, or even apartment properties, I would not recommend their stock except for amounts less than the government guarantee and preferably not then.

5. Loans. Personal unsecured loans should never be made, if there is any way to avoid making them. If the person requesting it is a friend, that is all the more reason for refusal. If you can afford to give him the money and want to make such a gift, very well. But never try to combine the elements of friendship and business. The friendship will end and the business element will be unsuccessful.

Mortgages are different

Mortgages are a different story. Since I cannot look over your shoulder in approving specific loans, let me suggest certain general rules: (1) The buyer should pay the expenses incident to the loan. These include a reasonable appraisal fee to a competent real estate man in estimating its present market value, the cost of bringing the abstract of title to date, examination by a good attorney of the title to see that it is free of objections, recording of the mortgage, escrow fees, if any, and insurance premiums; (2) The loan should never be made for more than 60 per cent of the appraised value; (3) Home loans should not be made except upon two and three bedroom houses in a good, young location—preferably upon houses of conventional architecture of pleasing design and, if possible, with a fair amount of brick or stonework. Seldom should loans be made upon very large houses, or in old locations which may deteriorate; (4) The mortgage payments and interest should be monthly, with reasonable forfeiture provisions; (5) The borrowers should be persons of good moral character; (6) A policy covering hazards of fire and other risks in excess of the amount of the loan should be taken in a reputable company, by the borrower, endorsed with a New York standard mortgage clause, and turned over to the mortgagee; (7) The mortgagee should record the mortgage, and retain the note, mortgage, abstract of title, and insurance policy in his safe deposit box.

6. Life insurance. Adequate insurance, of course, is a matter of common sense protection, but it is not designed primarily for investment income return. It may be utilized, as discussed previously, for the purpose of establishing a credit fund combined with estate protection.

7. Fear and off-trail investments. There are certain types of "fear" investments which are made by some people in the same sense of burying gold in the ground; others are freakish or off-trail purchases. They are not important in the sense of being common investments, but do deserve passing comment.

A. One of the most common of such purchases, since the hoarding of gold has become illegal, is the purchase of diamonds. This, it should be stated immediately, is a ghastly failure. A few of the reasons are: (1) Diamonds purchased at retail prices cannot be resold at retail prices, but only at wholesale or salvage values; (2) Like money, diamonds depreciate in dollar value in inflationary periods, causing a shrinkage of investment worth; (3) True it is that diamonds are portable but equally true is the fact that they are easily stolen. To protect them by insurance costs money, diminishing net value remaining; (4) Styles in cutting and shaping diamonds vary from one generation to another—and an obsolete method of cutting may make them unsalable without additional cutting, reducing the size of the jewel and necessitating more expense; (5) There are no earnings from such a frozen investment; (6) The present high value of diamonds is due to the fact that production is wholly controlled by a monopoly. If diamonds are ever found in substantial quantities elsewhere than in South Africa, and this is quite probable, values will drop sharply.

B. Other persons tie up surplus funds in works of art. From an investment point of view, value depends upon the

successful prognostication of the purchaser and upon changing trends in artistic appreciation. For example, the works
of Velasquez, Goya, Titian, Rembrandt, and some of the
early painters are now of tremendous value. In all likelihood,
they will not advance much more. By way of contrast, much
of the work of nineteenth century American artists, whose
fame reached great heights and whose works commanded
large sums a hundred years ago, are now wholly unpopular
and are considered mere daubs. The possessor of a museum
of such works will have lost a fortune. Of course, in another
fifty years, they may again become popular.

One of the most delightful hotels in which I have stayed
is the Ponce de Leon in St. Augustine. It, at least at the times
I stayed there, was owned by an estate and furnished largely
in the manner of the last century. Many of the paintings
which were popular fifty years ago hang upon its walls
now; and, while almost all of us shudder in horror at most
modern abstractions, it is easy to see how much really good
painting has progressed in that period of time. That is also
my reaction when I go through certain private museums
which specialize in the art popular in the last part of the nineteenth century. A few of the artists were outstanding; most
of them, even when well known, were inferior to the good
artists of today.

But is it art?

If one had visualized the future success of Picasso, he
could have realized a marked appreciation in value of his
investment. There are so many fads in art, and so many
changing concepts, that one must anticipate the waves of
the future. It is my own thought that future value of paintings will depend upon the following tests: (1) The painting
must be technically good. The artist must be respected as a
craftsman, and the picture appreciated for its skill, even by
excellent artists who represent wholly different schools of
thought. (2) It must be exciting. Many pictures exhaust

themselves when constantly viewed by one person. Unless it has such vitality that it can be seen daily, with constantly more affection, unless it can give the viewer an emotional lift, it is not great. (3) It must possess beauty. Pictures which are particularly revolting in subject matter, clash violently in their colors, or represent a mass of subconscious doodling of interest only to the painter or his psychiatrist, cannot reach heights of permanence. True, they may be museum pieces, since museums buy many god-awful paintings, but unless there is a great desire in individuals to own the work, there is no competition for its acquisition and no market value.

One who does intend to invest in works of art should know something about art—its history, trends, and techniques. He should know fine painters and teachers of art, and learn whom they respect. One man's opinion is not enough—particularly since there are violent clashes in art philosophy. But when he learns who are the artists' artists, at whose feet they sit to admire, the young artists whose techniques they compare with the greatest—those are the artists whom one should come to know. And then one should only buy such works as he personally loves. Then, assuming such artist is not discovered, and publicity passes him by, the investor has still bought beauty, he is surrounded by good art, and he will not lose.

One who has seen his movies would little suspect this, but Edward G. Robinson has been sensationally successful in art investments. He has possessed the faculty of selecting paintings for purchase which possess these germs of greatness. Yet, accordingly to him, he does not buy a painting unless it stirs him emotionally; and, if it lacks that power, he will not touch it. When he sold his art collection a few years ago, it returned many times its cost to him. Vincent Price, in more recent years, also has displayed the golden touch.

C. First editions of books are in a somewhat different position, although there are points of resemblance. The author, and the particular work, must possess intrinsic value. The number of copies available must be few. And, normally, the book must be in at least fair condition. Many bibliophiles prowl the stalls of secondhand bookstores looking for such treasures, and occasionally they succeed. It would seem that they would be equally successful in searching the tiers of books in small libraries of very old towns, and purchasing such books from the library boards.

D. Other persons, I am told, invest in original manuscripts. To predict which of these will increase in value, it seems to me, would require one to be an historian, a bibliophile, and a philosopher. Fred Fell, the publisher of this work, would fall into such a category, but not the author. This would require a degree of expertness for which few of us could qualify, and it is best to disregard any investment not within the field of our knowledge or experience.

E. Much more commonly, stamp collecting attracts many persons, young and old, looking for hobbies. The major field of stamp collecting is of United States commemoratives, although many persons purchase regular issues, air mails, special deliveries, or various types of domestic or foreign stamps. One who is interested in a very minimal savings program would find it possible to purchase issues of such stamps at par before they go off the market. After that time, those stamps may occasionally be found in some small post office; otherwise, they can be purchased only through stamp houses at an advance in price. If one does not overstock, such stamps cannot go below par, since they can always be used for postage. However, some business houses do buy such stamps at less than face value where collectors are forced to dump them for immediate cash. But the usual thing is that such stamps have a modest but steady advance in value. Most issues double in value within ten years from the time they go off the market, and some will advance much more markedly. Of course, if they are liquidated through a stamp house, that stamp house will want to make a profit upon its purchase, and some discount must be expected.

Tricks of the trade

At the present time, stamps are usually saved by collectors in blocks of four stamps—so as to show centering. Some collectors use panes of six. The investor should save the stamps in full sheets, since fads may change from one year to another. These should be kept in albums designed for that purpose, with the sheets separated by glassine to prevent sticking.

Stamps are judged as to value partially by the condition in which they are preserved and partially by centering. This refers to the position of the perforations between the stamps. If they cut into the designs, centering is "poor." If the perforations are exactly centered, this is "superb" and the stamps are of higher value. Centerline blocks, plate number blocks, or those with stamps containing an error are of greater value than more ordinary blocks.

Unless the buyer has excellent connections with the local post office which will notify him immediately when new stamps are received, and permit him to examine them at leisure, it is best to deal with the Philatelic Agency, Post Office Department, Washington 25, D. C. This bureau selects well-centered stamps for sale exclusively to collectors. One can write to it twice a year, secure lists of stamps then available, and order the new issues, or those about to go out of circulation. A good rule to follow, however, is for one starting such a plan not to become so enthusiastic personally about stamp collecting that he begins to buy stamps from dealers at premium prices. Our recommendation is not for the development of a hobby—it is a savings program only.

F. Others tend to go for coin collecting, upon which subject there is a great deal of literature. Since this requires an extensive knowledge of the nature of the coins collected, and often a considerable investment, it is well to do considerable preliminary study before embarking in this field. One of the most interesting hobbies of which I have heard recently, in this regard, is the collection of commemorative medals. Many of these were struck off in France during the Napoleonic era, and a good many others around the time of the Revolutionary War in this country. It can make a fascinating historical study, and I understand that many of these can be purchased at comparatively low cost. Actually, it brings an excellent form of art into the home at small expense. This is much more important than the savings or investment features.

G. One other thing should be mentioned because it has a certain fascination for some investors. That is the purchase of delinquent taxes. Every year, certain persons are late with tax payments. Usually, such delinquencies occur with reference to properties known as "junkers." However, the same situation sometimes arises in connection with rather good property. In many states, one may purchase the delinquent taxes and thereby become entitled to receive the same interest which otherwise would be received by the state or county (in some cases, 1 per cent a month) and all penalties (which may amount to 12 per cent to 24 per cent the first year). Usually, the purchaser also has a right to foreclose the tax liens if not repaid within a two-year period, if he has performed the statutory requirements; and occasionally property of value is so acquired.

This is a specialty all its own. Anyone planning to use such an investment should do three things: (1) He should have a long talk with a good real estate and tax lawyer in his state concerning the procedures and the dangers inherent in such purchases; (2) He should familiarize himself with the properties upon which he purchases the taxes; (3) He should check carefully to see that he fulfills all statutory requirements to protect his tax lien, and have each step checked by his attorney. Certainly, however, this must be regarded as an unorthodox type of investment, not to be used by the average or inexperienced person.

As we proceed with the further discussion on investments contained in the next few chapters, it is well to bear in mind the cautions contained in the beginning of this book. It must be remembered that the most important advice which can be given to any investor relates not to the making of money, but how to keep from losing money. More important than gaining an abnormal amount of financial security at an early age is the retaining of that security which is within one's grasp as he proceeds through life.

PRACTICAL POINTERS

1. Shoemaker, stick to your last. Some things in life are right for you and some are not. Weigh and measure before you embark on a career or invest your money.
2. Security grows as you grow older and you grow wiser. Take it easy.
3. Build a fund that is both inflation- and depression-proof; don't risk it through unfamiliar or crackpot investments.

2

The Stock Market: How to
Join Your Fortune
with America's

TELL YOU ALL ABOUT the stock market in one chapter? No.
But I have boiled down into this chapter the condensed experience of many stock traders and the advice of many books
—all about that huge area known as the stock market. More
important, perhaps, is a practical discussion of what makes
one stock a good investment and another a poor investment—
the reasons why some stocks climb in value while other decline. And while the purpose is not to make every man his
own broker, I do want to give you enough foundation so
that you can act with sound judgment.

I hope, in any case, this chapter shows you how closely
the stock market is tied to the growth of America. If you'll
see it that way, you'll concentrate on the word, *growth*.

If there is any one rule which is accurate, it is that most
people tend to invest at the wrong time. People are optimistic
and tend to buy on a booming market; they tend to sell

when the prices are depressed. This is a clear indication of the fact that they need help and guidance—but they need that guidance from conscientious persons engaged in that business, not from unsolicited literature which comes in the mail or from promoters interested in unloading a stock issue.

Another general rule which must be remembered is that as one seeks to enhance capital, risk increases. In other words, if all one is seeking is interest on his money, in a modest amount, he can do that with a fair degree of safety, although he is then subject to the vicissitudes of inflation. On the other hand, when he seeks to make his capital grow, he is then engaged in "risk-taking." The amount of risk may be comparatively small or comparatively great, but one must face the fact that there is an element of risk in all investments.

Be glad we outgrew the bad old days

If one had the necessary financial backing, in decades past it was possible for a financier to invest profitably in the market whether he was a "bull" or a "bear." The technique he employed was to buy up huge blocks of stock in a corporation, unload them to smash the market, and secretly buy them back together with other offerings which flooded the market in the resulting panic, induced by the reaction that I mentioned earlier that most people tend to sell when others are selling. Conversely, one might put in substantial bids for stock, increasing the price each time, buying the stock all along the line to force the price up and then unload at a marked advance. Rumors, whispering campaigns, and planted publicity all were used to promote the ends of the manipulator. However, these practices are illegal, and the New York Stock Exchange has ruled several stock issues off the Board entirely and prominent persons have, upon occasion, been indicted for alleged improper practices. Private issues still sometimes resort to artificial inflation practices—bringing out one issue at one dollar, a second at three dollars, a third at five dollars. Needless to say, such practices immediately constitute a red flag of danger.

The increasing control of the New York Stock Exchange over traders has been one reason why stock market prognostication has changed, in this instance, for the better. The second reason, which has affected stock market prognostication adversely, arises from present methods of government financing. We used to have a national government which spent little money. The first billion-dollar Congress adjourned in the 1920's. This was "one" billion dollars—not ninety or more billions. There was a treasury surplus. The amount of taxes was predictable. The value of a stock depended upon the balance sheet of the company, its earnings, dividends, and prospects. There were few unknown equations.

This is no longer true. The stock market fluctuates violently according to the action of our government and of other governments. A threat of war may send certain stocks skyrocketing, and depress the price of others. A change in the government interest rate affects the price of stocks and bonds alike. A corporation may commence to make substantial profits when, boom, comes another tax which cuts profits in half. This is bound to affect its dividends and, thus, the value of its stock. Or a substantial excise tax may be placed upon its product, reducing the market for such product, again cutting profits. The government may intervene in a strike and insist that the wages be raised, again cutting profits yet raising the price of the product which, in turn, reduces sales. Or Congress may pass a law or adopt an attitude toward business which creates a business set-back.

Let's see how the Wage and Hour law affected just one type of business. Western Union depended on large numbers of boys to deliver telegrams. The Wage and Hour law almost completely knocked out this method of operation. This, coupled with a recession, skidded its stock from above 90 (which was justified by earnings) to less than 20.

In 1957, the interest rate was increased by the government. This meant that money became tighter. When the interest rate increased, the value of government bonds issued at lower interest rates decreased. People desiring loans had to pay higher prices for them, and money became more scarce. The result was a retrenchment in certain types of activity, and a definite shift in the then-existing values of bonds and fixed-interest securities.

In considering the matter of investment in securities, one should never use his backlog for speculative purposes. It is neither wise nor fair to one's dependents to risk the funds needed for housing, food, clothing, and the like in an effort to gain wealth quickly. Keep a cushion. Don't place yourself in a position where one bad loss can ruin your entire financial position. This does not mean, however, that surplus funds should not be invested.

Money can be lost on the "gilt-edged"

But it is not, for example, ideal to put all of one's surplus funds into government securities. In the first place, the yield is low. In the second place, such yield as is realized from United States government securities is subject to income tax. In the third place, as inflationary trends continue, the purchasing power of that money may be cut in half. And, fourth, even government securities may shrink in value.

It has been possible, for example, to buy United States government securities, upon occasion, at prices as low as $75 for a $100 bond. This, of course, was most unusual; but it is not unusual to have United States government bonds drop from five to eight points as the interest yield upon new securities is changed. One cannot, therefore, buy any new form of United States government bond at 100 cents on the dollar when it is issued and expect to be able to liquidate that bond at any given time for that same figure. It may carry a premium or it may carry a discount.

The same is true of state municipal bonds. For example, as I stated previously, I bought five Illinois toll road bonds at 70. In a few months they rose about 10 points. From my point of view, they gave an excellent return, because it was income tax free, making the net income return to me worth approximately 12 per cent, taking income tax savings into consideration. Yet, when I bought at 70, this means that someone took a thirty-point loss upon bonds which were sold upon the basis of 100. Therefore, the mere fact that the securities are governmental in nature does not mean that they represent, under all circumstances, the ultimate in security.

There are similar disadvantages to industrial bonds, in that the dollar value remains fixed while the purchasing value of the dollar may be decreasing. There is, accordingly, a definite value to the investor in purchasing bonds which may be converted into common stock at a given price. The terminology usually used in this regard is "convertible debentures." These are simply notes or obligations of a corporation which may be converted into stock at a fixed price, thereby giving the owner of the bonds an opportunity to become part owner of the equity of the business if the upward movement of stock prices so warrants. This is an attractive double-feature type of security, which has a built-in elevator or elastic valve for the protection of the investor against continuing inflation.

A stock is not an obligation

When it comes to the purchase of stocks, we should understand what those securities represent. When we spoke of bonds, or debentures, we referred to indebtedness of the enterprise. A debenture is like a note, which is an obligation of the business normally repaid out of earnings, and bearing a fixed interest rate. Bonds are obligations which are normally secured by a mortgage. Stock, however, while the amount thereof is carried upon the debit side of the ledger, does not represent an obligation which must be repaid. That stands for the capital which has been invested by the people who, in effect, own the business. As earnings of the business increase and other obligations of the business are reduced, the value of the stock rises. Preferred stock may be limited in value, however, by reason of the fact that its earnings are usually limited, which means that the greatest opportunities for growth—but with less of a safety factor—are in common stock.

There are names that are commonly heard in reference to trading in securities. For example, one hears such terms as "blue chips," "cats and dogs," and "growth stocks." The terms are relatively self-explanatory. The blue chip stocks are comparatively safe, so far as possible insolvency of the company is concerned. Cats and dogs are wholly speculative —they may wash out tomorrow, or may make the holder thereof considerable sums of money. Growth stocks are those which usually pay small or no dividends, investing and rein-vesting the funds received in that industry itself in the hopes of a brighter tomorrow. That will be discussed more fully later.

There are investors, usually professionals, who buy for the "short term." Ordinarily this should not be less than six months, in any event, as the gain is otherwise treated as ordinary income instead of as a capital gain. Even there, the long-term investor may profit more in that, where stocks are held until the date of one's death, no capital gains tax is chargeable to the estate.

Short-term investment: leave it to pros

Ordinarily, a short term investment is based upon seasonal swings or fluctuations, and a long term investment is one reflecting a movement occurring over a long period of years. One who buys for the short pull must plan to spend an hour or more each day keeping abreast of current changes and in anticipating future dips and rises.

When Jean and I were first married, I had been studying the stock market professionally for several years, and making sufficient sums of money from it to retire college obligations. And, until the demands of my profession became sufficiently onerous to prevent such study, I supplemented my monthly income with as much or more each month from the stock market. However, in those instances, I used to watch carefully the general movements of all stocks and of particular issues, over a period of months and years, in charting their activities. There are, in general, seasonal trends—times of the year when stocks will drop several points, and times when there will be similar rises. Normally there will be a dip for year-end selling, a rise when dividends are declared. There may be other indications which will foretell that which is to come shortly thereafter—such as a change in interest rates, a sharp decrease or increase in freight car loadings, a sudden increase or drop in toll bridge revenues, and other indications.

As a general rule, one who follows seasonal trends, and this was true in my case, is required to chart the fluctuations of a particular stock and to learn its customary highs and lows during any given period. For example, a stock will frequently range, let us say, between 21½ and 28½. One constantly in touch with the situation will usually sell around 27½ to 28 and buy in at 22 to 22½—the differential constituting an excellent short-term profit. Another stock may vary from 68 to 83—with a median selling price of 75. This means that a sale well above this average is usually sound and a purchase well below the average is to be recommended. Of course, these suppositions exclude abnormal factors producing either inflationary or deflationary trends in the general market or with reference to the particular issue.

One thing which makes me shudder is when people ask me for recommendations as to a particular stock for them to purchase. If they would buy upon my recommendation, without more, they are speculators. In the early part of 1962, when I was expecting a sharp downturn in stock prices, a successful career woman of my acquaintance regaled me with the names of stocks which she had purchased and the paper profits which she had made, and wanted to know what securities I was purchasing. I told her flatly, "None," which surprised her, but I then explained that I did no purchasing except from the point of view of permanent investments.

During that same period, some lawyers in Illinois were telling me that they had formed a syndicate to buy "growth stocks," but that they had not been doing too well upon their investments. I asked them what securities they were purchasing, and it turned out that they were not buying growth stocks at all, but instead were buying well-traded stocks of mature companies of an entirely different type.

Inflation: Always with us

There is, accordingly, a complete lack of understanding upon the part of many persons as to the purpose of investment in securities. The purpose is to become a participant in the development of this nation. Progress could not be made in industry or commerce without investment capital. So long as progress is made, inflationary trends are going to continue, and those who own a part of American industry are going to increase their wealth proportionately.

★   *But each investor should be selfish enough to seek the maximum security possible for his capital, which requires buying for the long pull and outright ownership of the securities purchased. The small investor can never afford to buy on margin.*

Jean Paul Getty, believed to be the richest man in the world, has this to say about investing in the stock market:

"The Stock Market has a great appeal for men seeking wealth. Unfortunately, great numbers of them go into the market the wrong way. They want to speculate—not to invest. This is the worst possible approach.

"Selected common stocks are excellent investments. Stocks should be bought for investment, not speculation. They should be purchased when their prices are low and held for return and a long-term rise in value. I bought stocks during the Depression that are now worth 75 and 100 times what I paid for them! . . . .

"The selected—and I emphasize that *selected*—common stock is fine for investment. I'm certain of a market rise in the future. The Wall Street trend will definitely be *up* over the years—but, I repeat, stocks should be purchased and held, and not treated as purely speculative equities." *

We had a profesesor of mathematics at the University of Illinois, George Miller, who never made more than a small income. At the time of his death, he left a million dollars to the University. This had been acquired solely by long-term investments in securities. Such investments were not based upon speculation, but upon careful study of each security purchased, and with the guidance of professional investment counselors. And, even then, occasionally Professor Miller would get into an unprofitable or "sour" purchase. In such event, it is important that one have the good sense and courage to "cut his losses," by disposing of such issue and putting his money into a sound purchase which will give him an opportunity to recoup. The tendency of the average investor is to sell his good issues after they have made a profit and to keep the poor ones, which have declined. The professional investor does just the opposite. He gets rid of his lemons, takes a tax loss, and keeps the sound issues which just grow, and grow, and grow.

Your broker makes money when you "review"

One is frequently told that he should periodically review his investment program. There is some truth to that. But the investor must bear in mind that an unscrupulous stock broker may seek to have him review his program merely for the

* *True, The Man's Magazine,* June, 1958.

purpose of encouraging him to sell certain issues which have made a profit and to purchase others, for the sake of the commissions which will inure to such broker. Fortunately, most investment counselors are not of that type, and will encourage the investor to retain any sound issue which has excellent future potential. There is another disadvantage in constantly reviewing one's position, in that it often creates a tension in persons to observe the changes in a stock market picture, particularly if they have been adverse. And anyone who invests in securities must, from time to time, expect adverse periods.

The truth is that if the investment was sound to start with, there is no reason to dispose of it. If the corporation is sound, well-managed, paying dividends through thick and thin, with a constant income, and with a good future, it should usually be retained. Every switch in a security which one makes costs him brokerage fees and income taxes. Therefore, except for switching out of situations which have reaped their complete potential, or which have lost their promise, long-term ownership is generally to be preferred.

What about mutual funds?

Now the small investor cannot secure a spread—that is, a diversification in many lines of enterprises. He can do this to some degree through investments in mutual fund shares or in investment syndicates—some of which specialize in one type of security, others of which hold a wide diversification of all types of shares. Their fluctuation reflects directly the fluctuations in their holdings.

Mutual funds have certain shortcomings from a growth point of view. They are also subject to some criticism by reason of expense in the acquisition of business and the administration of it. However, they do have certain definite advantages. (1) Such a fund can give a diversification of first-class industries, many of the so-called gilt-edged or blue-chip variety; (2) it gives a professional supervision of an investment program, thus preventing an investor from losing his financial security by acting on hot tips; (3) it creates an enforced savings program, encouraging the investor to accumulate funds which he might otherwise spend. By siphoning off certain regular amounts each month, it creates almost painlessly an investment program which otherwise might never be realized.

It is difficult for a small investor otherwise to secure such a diversification. If that individual prefers to buy stocks in certain corporations directly, it is a mistake to buy one or two shares in a number of corporations in trying to achieve that objective. The brokerage fees upon purchases and sales of this type may completely eat up any gain which might be realized from an advancement in price. While there are many who object to "putting all their eggs in one basket," it seems to me better to put their eggs in one or two good baskets, if necessary, and to keep their eyes upon that basket. If possible, it is well to buy and sell in lots of an even 100 shares, since that avoids a charge of one-eighth each way upon purchases and sales which is customary in odd-lot transactions. Thus, if one wants to sell 50 shares of a stock at 40, the selling price must be 40⅛ in order for him to realize his asking price.

So you want to buy a stock

Let us assume that we are contemplating a purchase of a stock and selecting it personally, with the idea of keeping our eyes on that basket. The first thing I would do is look over the list of securities available. One can secure a Standard & Poor or Fitch stock record which lists all actively traded stocks, their financial structures, annual earnings for a period of years, dividends, price fluctuations, etc.

In certain cases, such as steel, utilities, and other industries requiring huge fixed assets and liabilities, the following test cannot be used. Normally, however, in other instances, I want "cash and equivalent" to be at least double that of all "current liabilities," and "current assets" to be at least four times the amount of "current liabilities"—substantially more if there is a wide variation in the market for the product of the particular industry in times of depression. If the industry is of a particularly safe type, the ratio of cash to current liabilities may be smaller.

At the time of writing this chapter for the first edition of this book in 1958, I used Eastman Kodak as an illustration. At that time, its cash and equivalent was $168,000,000; current assets $417,000,000; and current liabilities $122,000,000. The ratio is now $300,000,000 cash and equivalent; current assets $616,000,000; and current liabilities $204,000,000. Both then and now the ratio was satisfactory for a major industry.

At that time, I pointed out that its annual earnings per share were: 1952—$2.74; 1953—$2.86; 1954—$3.99; 1955—$4.66; 1956—$4.89; 1957—$5.09. It has since split 2 shares to 1, but the same modest growth has continued, the earnings on the split stock being: 1958—$2.57; 1959—$3.24; 1960—$3.30; 1961—$3.88; 1962—$3.65. Of course, others feel this to be a rather promising investment also, so that the present selling price is high compared to earnings or to dividend return.*

Important questions

I then ask such questions as these. What is the type of industry? Is it one which will continue to grow and develop with our economy? The answer here is obviously yes. Next, for how long a period of time has it paid dividends without interruption? Checking this, I find that dividends have been paid every year since 1902. That is a good indication that it weathered two depressions without even interrupting its dividend payment, which means some stability of income production, even in bad times. If I want further information

---

* Eastman, then selling at around 100, has since split 2 for 1 with an adjusted price of around 160 at the old ratio (around 80 following the split, at the time this chapter is being written).

concerning its management, its balance sheets, and other factors indicative of its future, I can ask my stock broker to get that information for me and he will be glad to do so.

At the time of such last writing, I also mentioned Sterling Drug, Inc., which had demonstrated a modest, but steady, increase in adjusted earnings from 1952 to 1957 of $1.32 to $2.35. Since 1957, that same gradual increase has been maintained, climbing in 1958 from $2.42, 1959 to $2.65, 1960 to $2.80, 1961 to $2.95, and 1962 to $3.11. Utility stocks of companies located in growing communities often combine a like modest growth with reasonable safety. On the other hand, companies whose earnings fluctuate violently, or decline steadily are not recommended for the conservative investor.

Keep your eye on revenue

Of course, the income from any stock could still make the price attractive, unless the stock is bought purely for growth purposes. Even then, there must be a reasonable relationship between net earnings and selling price. The purpose of owning any investment is for the production of revenue—and, if it cannot produce revenue commensurate with the price it commands, there is something wrong. For example, in the bull market of 1929, stock purchases upon margin drove the price of some securities up to a point where the earnings were not over one per cent of the selling price at a time when such earnings were at the very peak. This is, of course, ridiculous.

The purchaser must also consider the type of business as it relates to our general economy, and the position of that particular enterprise. Is the type of industry which it represents, first, a dying business? In certain instances, new techniques, equipment, and products may render an industry wholly or partially obsolete. True, an enterprising concern will modify its techniques and take on new activities, but others may wither on the vine. This must be carefully evaluated. Manufacturers of buggies, horse collars, and feed bags found themselves in a declining economy after the automobile became popular. At the present time, electronics, automation, and those industries dealing with new types of minerals and derivatives therefrom may be in the ascendancy. The investor must use his sound judgment as to the future of the industry in general.

In addition, not all securities are affected alike by economic cycles. Some are greatly accelerated, while others are retarded, by war. When building and heavy manufacturing boom, steel is in demand but people smoke only a few more cigarettes. In depression times, they continue to smoke but steel demands are low. Not all stocks move with the same impetus with an identical stimulus.

The continuity of a business must be considered. Certain short line railroads are tremendously valuable, for example, because they lead directly from mines to mills, are constantly busy, and have a large tonnage with little wastage. Other railroads must depend upon a vastly fluctuating business—being rushed during harvesting season and high industrial periods, and being operated non-profitably during many other times.

A business is made or un-made by men

One must look to the management and to company policy. If the corporation is family controlled, beware! Papa's death may play havoc with it. If it is the type of concern which fails to take young men into positions of responsibility, and which is dominated by old or timid management, again one must beware. Sometimes a crisis will arise when one old man dies, when a major shakeup of company policy arises. Management is too vital a part of the financial picture to overlook.

One must also consider what particular difficulties may be presented with reference to any particular business. For example, let us suppose that a corporation has large holdings in the Middle East, in Central America, or in Asia. War, or threats of war, may largely reduce its income, or even result in the confiscation of such properties. This was true when Hitler, for example, in the 1930's, confiscated substantial holdings of corporations having interests in Europe.

There are factors also to be considered with reference to each particular corporation. For example, I have been told that one sulphur company has seriously depleted its natural resources. This, of course, would be a factor affecting the sound value of its stock; and, even though merely a rumor, would bear detailed and accurate checking. I am familiar with two different copper companies, one of which has a much lower unit cost of production than the other, which means that the profits of the first should be much more substantial. In any mineral, or oil, situation, one should familiarize himself with the total reserves held by that company, the steps which it takes to add to its reserves, its unit cost of production, and the competency of its management.

When to ignore the financial news

If one buys for the long pull, not intending to sell upon price advances, he need not keep abreast of general stock market movements. And that is advisable. As a matter of fact, if one reads an item in the newspaper which either encourages him or alarms him with reference to a particular industry, it is already then too late to buy or sell upon the basis of that information. The insiders know those factors which influence favorably or unfavorably the financial picture of a corporation. They either buy up heavily of the stock in question or quietly unload. Six months later, when the general public learns of these matters, the price has already readjusted to take care of the situation. The reaction of the impulse buyer or seller is far too late.

My own preference in the purchase of stocks—and I think the same thing should be true of any purchaser less than fifty years of age, except a widow dependent upon income—is for growth securities. That is a term which is much

abused and much misunderstood. Precisely what is meant
by it?

★   *A growth security refers to the type of industry which may pay small or no dividends but
which plows back its earnings into the production
of new business and in which a constantly increasing market may be expected, with a commensurate increase in size of the organization.*

At the time of last writing, I used as an illustration
Smith, Kline & French Laboratories, of which the earnings
climbed from $0.90 in 1952 to $4.24 in 1957. It then split
3 for 1, but its earnings continued to increase, on a more
modest basis, from $1.43 in 1958 to $2.08 in 1962.

Ethical drug stocks, however, well may be in the doldrums
for some years to come. It is recognized by physicians that
there is some risk to all medications. Penicillin, which annually saves the lives of tens of thousands, kills a few each year
who are allergic to it. However, because of the thalidomide
catastrophe certain Congressmen, the late Estes Kefauver
in particular, proposed to strip the profit from drugs by
shortening the patent period to three years—directly dis-
couraging new research by eliminating the profit motive.
Also, the new F.D.A. regulations are so onerous that they
destroy the small laboratory, which cannot afford the tremendous expense of qualifying. It is the small laboratories of
past decades that grew into the giants of today.

Granted that reasonable regulation is necessary, over-
regulation can destroy this industry and prevent new and
useful discoveries, even as it has in Mexico. Until a period
of greater normalcy is reached, then, I cannot recommend
pharmaceutical stocks as investments.

Another type of growth concern is a relatively new business represented here by Revlon, which spends tremendous
amounts of money in advertising. These amounts are, of
course, deductible from income as business expenses; yet

such advertising greatly increases the gross revenue and, in turn, the size of the concern. The difficulty is that where the growth factor is dependent upon advertising, the nature of the market created is somewhat artificial, and a sudden loss of popularity of any product could drop it sharply. The growth of the drug and chemical industry is sounder, in that regard.

It happened before, it can happen again

To give some illustrations of comparative growths, in 1943, $10,000 invested in General Electric would by 1955 have been worth $45,400, in addition to paying dividends of approximately $9,500. $10,000 invested in Dow Chemical, at that same time, would have been worth $49,000 in 1955, in addition to paying dividends of approximately $6,000. $10,000 then invested in International Business Machines had increased in value by 1955 to $100,000, in addition to paying dividends of $8,000. Of course, while these industries were making substantial gains, some others were standing still or even retreating.

But there is another type of growth investment which, taken on a national level, far outshines the industrial. I refer to stock life insurance companies. Some investments in the life insurance industry have been phenomenally productive. For example, $1,000 invested in National Life and Accident Insurance Company of Nashville, Tennessee, in 1905, would presently be worth $400,000. Taking an even shorter period, the period from 1943 to 1955 which I mentioned earlier, a $10,000 investment in Aetna Life would in twelve years have grown to $125,000; $10,000 in Continental Assurance to $325,000; and $10,000 in Lincoln National to $524,000 —none of these counting the dividends which would have been received in those periods, and in each instance these exceeded the original purchase price. Some years ago, $1,000 invested in Franklin Life increased to almost $50,000 in a little over two years; and $1,000 invested in Philadelphia Life increased to $95,000 in less than three years. I know one physician who has based his entire investment program, for some years, in life insurance stocks.

Here are a few of the reasons why life insurance stocks can be better than industrial, or even other insurance, stocks.

1. The life insurance premium averages out larger compared to, let us say, the automobile, fire, or hospitalization premium. Therefore, a company receiving larger average premiums should grow faster with the same number of policyholders.

2. The commission paid to agents—although quite substantial the first year and with some renewal commissions for a limited number of years—averages out lower than other insurance forms where the commission continues at a level rate every year the insurance is renewed.

3. Life insurance continues in force for a longer period. Rarely does a person carrying life insurance cancel it, whereas other forms of insurance may be switched from company to company every few years. A life policy usually continues in force from twenty to thirty years.

4. The administration and claims costs are lower. It doesn't take much personnel per dollar of premium to send out premium notices and to credit funds received or to pay a death benefit. However, an automobile policyholder may have numerous small claims or a real stinger which involves a bulky claims file and possibly even defense of a suit in court.

5. Since our emphasis in life insurance is upon safety, so that funds will be present to pay death benefits, the rate structure is geared to provide adequate reserves. These have in them a growth factor because, first, longevity continues to improve, with a premium charge based upon present mortality tables; second, earnings on investments, in this day of high interest rates, is greater than originally projected.

6. Inflation makes for growth in the life insurance industry. It was once considered a mark of wealth to leave an insurance estate of $25,000. A person in present comparable

status may now carry $100,000 or more. And with insurance of wives, children, pension plans, and other forms becoming more widely utilized, the gross total of insurance in force tends to increase constantly. The amount of life insurance per family trebled from 1943 to 1958.

7. There is a constant roll-over as to insurance in force. An agent sells Mr. Smith. Mr. Smith's policy remains in force for thirty years, so the agent in succeeding years sells Mr. Brown, Mr. Jones, and Mr. Miller. In addition, as any one insured dies, others take his place. In fact, the children of each insured, as they become adults, become potential buyers, so that as the population increases there simply are more persons insured.

But this very bonanza available through life insurance stocks—the occasional pot of gold at the end of the rainbow —has set the stage for a regular game of widow clipping. A few weeks ago, young widow Avery (let's call her that) phoned me. I had just recovered a little over $20,000 for her arising out of her husband's death. A life insurance stock salesman was at her home to transfer her dollars into certificates of his company.

She didn't buy—not after I had talked to her. And neither should you, certainly not the promotional issues. In fact, ordinarily you shouldn't buy the stock of any company which is less than six years old. Once in a while you'll pass up a potential profit. But you'll also pass up a lot of potential losses—particularly in the area of any insurance stocks.

For example, a number of folks in this county invested in a company called Illini Auto. It grew rapidly: in fact, it secured more than a million dollars of premium income—of business other companies didn't want. The company had no trained underwriter, actuary, or administration. The same was true of Mid-Union Indemnity, of Elgin, which took on long-haul truck business, a specialized risk. Both are now bankrupt. I have a judgment of $200,000 on behalf of some clients against one insurance man who has been identified with five unsuccessful companies. And, at the time of this writing,

Central Casualty Company of Evanston, with over two million dollars of annual premium income, is being liquidated. The foregoing were not life companies, but similar examples involving life companies can also be given.

This does not mean that all insurance companies are prone to failure. Far from it! This is an excellent and well-policed industry. But these illustrations, and I could give many more, show that an investment poured into a company which may "go bust" isn't likely to buy ale and pretzels in your sunset years. And perhaps fifteen out of sixteen new companies are "hesitant Harrys" instead of the "booming bonanzas."

That's pretty poor odds for speculation, laddie—one chance out of sixteen, if you don't know what you're doing. And this is more true in the last few years than ever before. Why?

Primarily, there are two reasons. One is that the fantastic potential of life insurance stock investments is just beginning to be realized. As a result, many people who want to get rich (particularly on other people's money) start new companies.

Many of these are started by insurance agents who see the bonanza possibilities but don't realize that it takes much more than their highly trained blarney to make a company prosper. It takes a great knowledge of insurance contract needs and knowledge of how to design contracts to fill those needs; it requires actuarial skill, sound underwriting and claims practices, and good company administration. Rarely can an insurance salesman supply all of these needs.

Again, many such companies are started by promoters. In past years, Texas, Indiana, and Illinois have been the worst offenders. Some companies were formed by promoters purely to reap the commission on stock sales. More often, the promoters will take the first issue at a low price per share—perhaps 15c to 35c a share. They then put out a first public issue at $3 a share, a second at $5 a share, a third at $7.50. The little larceny in the heart of each buyer leads him to believe that some third guy will pay him still more for his stock—

while the promoters quietly unload their holdings privately at ten times or twenty times what they paid and walk away from any further responsibility.

The state insurance departments are concerned about this—gravely concerned. Illinois, for example, is putting a stop to such practices in part by requiring the promoters' stock to be held in escrow until it is worth the public issue price. But the very existence of these shares still dilutes the value of all the stock, so that the $7.50 stock probably is worth about $1.00—as a pure speculation. And I wouldn't buy it at that price.

Ordinarily, life insurance companies must operate in the red for a minimum period of three to five years while developing an agency force, evolving a sound method of operation, and making their early mistakes. During the six years I mentioned, the shaking down process should have ended and a sound growth basis established, if the company then is still in business. At the end of that time, if you have to pay a premium to buy the stock, the added cost is well worth while. That's when growth can really begin, if you have picked your company well.

How does one pick out a life insurance company with real growth potential, yet possessing maximum safety? It would help, of course, if one knows the industry in general and the management of any suggested company. But here are certain tests to apply:

1. What is its book value per share? Take the number of shares divided into its combined capital and surplus. This will not reflect the value of business on the books, but the stock should not sell for ten times that net book value. It may sell for three to five times that figure, however, if it is a rapidly growing company.

2. Is it operating profitably? If its annual operations are "in the red"—as they are in its initial years, leave it alone. Let it emerge from its swaddling clothes. Otherwise, it is a speculation, not an investment.

3. At what rate has capital and surplus increased over

the last ten years? It should at least have doubled—and some will do much better.

4. Is it steadily increasing the volume of "permanent" business each year? If it produced, in millions per successive years, 6, 8, 12, 14, 18, 26, 32—that shows progressive management.

5. What is the rate of growth of total business in force? It means nothing for a company to do a tremendous business each year if the total insurance in force does not increase. The total should be increased by at least 60 per cent of the last year's business, after crediting normal lapses and deaths of policyholders.

6. Don't buy stock of a company having assets of less than four million dollars (it is too speculative) or over fifty million dollars (or its greatest growth may be behind it). The most rapid rate of growth usually will happen to a company having assets of between ten and twenty million if it has already shown a capacity for rapid and sound growth.

Given the above rules, it is simple to compute the book value of a company by taking the total number of shares and dividing this into the combined capital and surplus. A solid company operating in the black may be selling for three times, or a little more, than this figure. Some which have demonstrated fantastic growth potential have sold as high as ten times book value—although one should weigh the relationship of book value to potential growth carefully in selecting which stock to buy, since there are always good, moderately young, progressive life insurance companies meeting my tests.

On the other hand, this demonstrates quite clearly that a spanking new company, operating at a deficit, with a book value of $0.70 a share cannot support a market price of $12 a share, as is true of one company recently brought to my attention.

Value depends on circumstances

There are some organizations which have formed syndicates for the holding of just such stocks. This manages to give some spread or diversification of those holdings. Otherwise, one must rely upon his investment counselor checking the backgrounds of new, young, vigorous, and well-managed life insurance companies after they have given proof of their stability.

When one purchases a true growth stock, it does not make too much difference as to the price at which he purchases it. If he has correctly evaluated its possibilities, despite temporary retreats in price, such a stock will continue to forge ahead and to become valuable as time goes on. That is not necessarily true in the case of other securities. In those situations, whether one has made a good investment or a bad investment may depend entirely on whether it is bought at a high price or at a low price. Certain stocks do well in periods of high production and often fare badly during depressions.

Steel stocks, for example, are inflationary and war babies. Motors, accessories, mining stocks, and many railroads have a similar financial history, and should be bought during periods of depressed economic situations. On the other hand, drugs, retail stores, snuff and tobacco, sulphur, and match stocks do not accelerate their earnings to any great degree during prosperity nor are they as hard hit during times of depression. Usually, therefore, at the peak of inflationary periods it may be well to switch out of inflationary type securities. However, after a depression has existed for several years and those stocks have paid no dividends from earnings, and show large annual deficits, their prices may become very attractive.

It is not, of course, a simple matter to predict when a depression will occur. Sometimes, such an occurrence can be postponed. Again, the effects may be minimized. We must remember, however, that the basic principles of the laws of economics do operate, and some of these we should consider in making an effort to evaluate the future of investments in this nation.

A look at some basic angles of our

economy

From approximately 1930 to 1938, there was almost no building in the United States although the population continued to increase. There were few automobiles and few appliances, which means a huge backlog of housing, automobiles, and appliances was building up. From approximately 1938 to 1941, these industries progressed in a rather active manner.

However, war came in 1941, and no new automobiles were built, no homes, and no appliances. There was a tremendous surge in population resulting from the vast crop of war babies, which means that the back orders which had already accumulated were given a terrific upsurge. When 1946 and peace came, there was a vast accumulation of back orders in all fields of consumer spending, and people had plenty of money. Those who had not been to war had substantial savings from high salaries; the returned veterans normally had accumulated substantial overseas pay and bonuses. There was both high government and high private spending.

It is apparent, however, that people do not need two homes to live in. They do not buy new stoves or new refrigerators to replace those which are working capably, merely because of slight style changes. Eventually, therefore, they get caught up, to a degree. Government spending cannot replace orders for automobiles, stoves, refrigerators, radios, and television sets.

Normally, it is expected that in boom times, such as we

experienced after the close of World War II, the government spending will be cut to a minimum. In such periods, it is expected that substantial payments will be made to reduce government obligations and to lessen the interest which will accumulate thereon. However, with the Korean War and the constant cold war which has been waged by Russia in order to drive America to bankruptcy, through excessive foreign aid and domestic spending, no such opportunity has arisen. Instead, the government debt has constantly increased, entailing high annual expenditures for interest alone. There is no government reserve, then, to produce prosperity in the event a depression period should come about.

Let us go back to fundamentals. Ordinarily, if the average amount of government spending were ten billion dollars a year in normal times, and a depression came about, we would expect to double or triple such government spending in public work projects for a two-fold purpose: first, to build substantial public works, such as buildings and highways, at a time when cost is low; second, to provide work to take care of the unemployed, rather than using a "dole." However, if the average governmental budget is a hundred billion dollars, and it takes all of the taxable income to meet that figure in boom times, then when income is greatly reduced during periods of depression, the governmental income is necessarily much less. Thus, if the governmental income during such a year is sixty billions, it could not even continue the rate of spending it has had previously except by incurring a substantial debt.

And the question arises: "Who can buy the forty billion dollars worth of new bonds?" For, in such times, everyone's pockets seem to be sewn shut.

Are we looking for trouble?

That situation is alarming. Partially to offset it, there is the factor of our constantly increasing population. Even though one family does not need two houses, or four automobiles, nevertheless there are new families coming along who do need homes. This type of demand would not, in any one year, offset the shrinkage in back orders of long standing, but they will create new business of all types. This applies to homes, automobiles, appliances, furniture, clothing, food, and all other products of our economy. There is definitely a rapid population surge. Whereas in the depression of the 1930's, people tended to marry late and to have few children, the tendency now is for couples to marry early and to have large families. The present population boom unquestionably will have an effect of an inflationary nature upon our economy.

The fears as to the solidity of our national economy are not held by this writer alone. Government economists are quite aware of that situation. It is apparent that since the national debt will not be reduced in dollars, it must be reduced in practical effect. The only way this can be done is by increasing cheapness of the dollar. For example, if the governmental income should double, by reason of the fact that average incomes double, then the debt seems to be only half of what it was before. This means that those who have investments in government bonds, or other fixed dollar credits, suffer. But that seems to be the natural trend of our economy—and it seems to be inevitable. With that in mind, it is well to remember that there may, at any time, be recessions whenever back orders for goods, merchandise, and housing have been filled. There may be a real belly-busting depression if the filling of such back orders, discharge of employees, reduction in government income, and reduction in government spending all occur simultaneously. But, if these various factors are staggered, in the intervals in which they occur, then it is apparent as to what the tentative remedies will be. And it appears inevitable that we will continue to have a rising spiral of prices, wages, and inflation, with a resulting cheapening of the dollar, requiring a person to look for sound growth investments which will maintain or even increase the dollar reserves which he possesses. But it would seem a part of sound public policy to cut government expenditures in boom times in order to maintain a cushion for the less plentiful periods.

Concern must be expressed also over competition from other nations whose factories were built with American dollars—and which now undersell us, creating a constant outflow of gold in addition to that which we pour out in foreign aid. Both political parties are equally at fault in these respects. The only note of promise upon the economic horizon is the present cut in personal income taxes in the higher brackets which may restore earning incentive and help to create new employing entitities. Risk capital is discouraged when the potential for profit disappears.

The other markets

In addition to dealing upon the New York Stock Exchange it must be recognized that there are other markets— such as the American Stock Exchange (formerly called the "Curb"), the Midwest Stock Exchange, the Toronto Stock Exchange, and many others—with some of the best purchases appearing, from time to time, on "over the counter" transactions. However, those transactions require much more detailed investigation, since information about those companies is not public information to the same degree as in the case of major corporations.

Other persons make livelihoods dealing in the grain or commodity markets. These are transactions which involve betting on whether the price of the grain or the commodity will go up or down. It is different from purchasing a stock in respect to the fact that one does not anticipate acquiring and holding the commodity or grain—at least, not for an indefinite time.

One may well expect to own a stock permanently, riding

it through boom times and bad. Since the commodity transactions involve dealing in futures—that is, predicting the
price at which something will sell at a different time—it is
not to be recommended for the average investor. Only the
man of considerable experience in those markets is consistently
successful—and even many such investors guess wrong.

Upon the financial or money markets, government controls prevent a degree of manipulation which used to be
quite common. Frequently, twenty years and more ago, a
differential would exist in the rate of exchange between two
nations. With no limitations upon currency export and im-
port, the financier in this country would, let us say, buy
bills of exchange upon Spain. An assistant in Spain might
buy like bills upon Brazil, and an assistant there might buy
them upon the United States—with a differential of 10 per
cent upon the complete transaction. Again, this is not for
the average investor, and circumstances completely beyond
the money market may now cause violent fluctuations
therein.

It is to be seen from the foregoing that anyone who seeks
to invest must combine his own wisdom with that of experts
in attempting to invest soundly, rather than to speculate.
Only in this way can he hope to make himself both inflation-
proof and deflation-proof.

The Small Business Corporation Act

One of the best investments in this present period of our
economy is in corporations formed under the Small Business
Investment Company Act. Briefly, the purpose of such companies is to finance new enterprises on a basis where the
SBIC receives "debt-type" documents representing the advance, plus a percentage of common stock in the new
company as a bonus. Under sound management which selects
such enterprises carefully, and helps to guide them during
their formative periods, the growth potentials in both the
SBIC and its protégé are enormous. And, from the viewpoint

of the high-income investor, there is an added attraction inducing the creation of an SBIC. Ordinarily, the investor may not charge off investment losses which exceed gains of more than $1,000 a year. The losses he may charge off in investments made under this statute are not limited. To be blunt, if his corporation wins, he wins; if it goes *kaput*, Uncle Sam takes most of the loss. Yet it is a good statute, since it gives those who have funds available to invest an incentive to create new businesses which are important to our national economy; new employment opportunities are created, and new customers for materials and services. The results have been to increase, not to decrease, total income taxes collectible.

PRACTICAL POINTERS

1. Tailor your investment program to fit your needs.
2. As opportunity for gain increases, so almost always does risk increase. Never forget this, especially when someone tells you he has found an exception.
3. Don't use your backlog for speculation. (Don't go to sea without a life preserver.)
4. Don't: A. Buy on tips
             B. Buy "cats and dogs"
             C. Buy for the short term
5. Before you invest, find out all you can about the company that interests you. Consider, too, the industry that company represents.
6. Select growth-type stocks from industries with a brilliant potential. The time you spend finding them can pay off better than any other hours of your life.
7. Keep an eye on the general economy. It tells a story, if you will listen.

3

You Can Make Money by
Buying In

You CAN, indeed, make lots of money by the buying-in process. We'll take a look, in this chapter, at some well-known
people who made money not only by direct business acumen
but by means of acquiring a whole or part interest in something that was "going for a song."

You'll see, however, that the ability to shop for a bargain
is only half the story. If you buy a business cheap, it is not
likely to do you much good unless you have a workable plan
for managing it, reorganizing it or otherwise handling it so
that soon it is worth more. There are many angles. We'll
look into the best of them.

Then too there is the magic that hangs on the word
"control." What is control? How do you get it? How can
one company control another, then perhaps another and
another? And how can a mere option—not in itself very
expensive—give you control over property worth millions

and the ability to siphon a percentage into your own pocket?

Such matters are not only for financiers. High-level or low-level, the principles work when you know how to work them.

You may, for instance, know a man who keeps cash always handy. The reason is that he can jump in where money is urgently needed and come out with an excellent return with perhaps a piece of a good business in the bargain.

When money was insecure in Germany, after World War I, the financier Leopold Silberstein—then a young man—bought up real estate. In terms of the devaluating currency his property doubled, quadrupled in value and then was the only thing to retain value. Later he was in China where money was scarce. Having money, he entered the banking business.*

Find a man who has brains, ability and money sense, and you can make substantial sums by backing him. For example, you may know a young man who has prodigious energy and a worthwhile idea, but he may lack the money to get his enterprise underway. However, there is an income tax danger in backing such a venture, because if it proves unsuccessful the loss therefrom may be limited to $1,000 in any one year.

One of the main faults of the young businessman, outside of over-enthusiasm for an untried venture and the failure to realize the pitfalls therein, is in being undercapitalized. When this happens, others may step in and take over. As was well stated by Price A. Patton:

"Another investment possibility, usually offering high return possibilities with a big element of risk, is financial participation in a new business venture. A tremendous percentage of new businesses are marked for failure before they start. The biggest single cause of these failures is lack of money-management ability. I have been asked to look into many hopeless situations where the floundering

* *Operation Success,* pp. 16, 23.

business could have been saved sixty days earlier by sound management of money. The technical ability, or production experience, or merchandising knowledge of the owner was adequate and the initial success of the venture promising, but early success is a concealed trap. There are always plenty of people to help an optimistic new business overstock, over-equip, over-advertise, over-produce and over-borrow. If you want to put money into any business, even an established one, learn something about the ability of the management in money matters." *

There are these risks which Mr. Patton points out. On the other hand, for the seasoned businessman, who understands that type of business, his investment may have a two-fold purpose: first, he may rescue a fledgling business, preventing insolvency and keeping it alive for the rendition of a worthwhile service; second, as the rescuer, he is certainly entitled to adequate compensation for the risk which he takes. Furthermore, to assure it against falling into similar financial traps or mismanagement in the future, he will want a reasonable interest in the enterprise and is entitled to it. Relatively small amounts of money can swing great weight at the right time. The power of money to make money depends on the situation and the timing. Hold your resources for that place and that moment when they will explode in value.

Property too can pay off the same way

But, instead of investing in a new business, one may choose to acquire property—either as tangible property, as intangible property representing an interest in a different kind of property, or in the form of a toehold in business. For example, wherever there is a substantial estate, usually there are substantial obligations to be paid either to creditors or by way of tax claims of the state or Federal government.

* Price A. Patton and Martha Patton, *Freedom from Money Worries,* Fawcett Publications, Inc., copyright, 1958, p. 153.

In such event, property belonging to the estate must ordinarily be sold. The same situation arises in connection with corporate receiverships, bankruptcies, and other court proceedings. Sometimes farm land is involved. At a private sale, a bargain may result—but, at a public auction, spirited bidding from neighbors may carry the price beyond its true value. In the case of a residence, frequently a depressed price will purchase the property at either type of sale. The smart commercial buyer usually will repair and redecorate the property and sell it immediately after the six-month period has run for capital gains advantages, or use it for purposes of exchange to avoid income tax entirely.

Build in a margin for error

Occasionally one will purchase all of the personal property en masse. The furniture can be sold to dealers, sometimes turning up an antique of value; a good original painting, valuable jewelry, or even worthwhile unlisted securities may appear. The buyer should always make a careful examination of all property so offered, appraise it mentally upon a conservative basis, and never offer more than half that amount. The difference is his margin for error, payment for his time, and profit.

Both in estates of deceased persons, and in receiverships, large blocks of securities occasionally turn up. The persons concerned are reluctant to dump a large block of stock upon the market which will depress the price. This may mean a sale to a private individual at considerably less than market price—with the buyer either retaining such holdings for the long pull, or feeding it gradually into the market for sale.

One of the most striking illustrations of this coming to my attention was with reference to the old Cord Corporation and its successor holding companies, Aviation & Transportation, Inc., Aviation Corporation, and the like. The holding company held control, through a large block of stock, of Auburn Auto. Auburn Auto had in its portfolio a huge block of stock in Aviation Corporation. So, in 1938, Auburn Auto was put through the wringer and a petition was filed with the bankruptcy court for authority to sell all the stock it held in Aviation Corporation as a block. My recollection may be slightly off as to the precise amounts, but the sale price was around one dollar a share while it was then selling on the market for around three and a half.

This sort of thing often results because of the "blockage rule" in connection with taxes. If 500 shares of stock in a corporation are sold, the price of the stock upon the market will not vary. This is particularly true if there are buyers available for 2,500 shares. The old law of supply and demand dictates that the potential buyers will keep the price up. But, if there are 50,000 shares of stock to be sold, then the buyers have a field day, because they can buy at a far lower price. Even the government recognizes this, and, where a large block of stock exists, recognizes that dumping it upon the market will depress the price of the stock. Furthermore, in such sales as I have mentioned, it costs money to liquidate a particular security; in addition, frequently the statutes require that the method of sale be by public bid or sealed bid. When this is the situation, it is perfectly proper to seek to buy the property at the lowest price at which it can be secured.

Of course, before you buy you must know the value of what you are buying or you have no standard against which to measure. You must know that there is a market where you can resell—*at a profit*. Then, not a year later. You have to keep money moving, ordinarily, to make it valuable; and a year's pace could change a bargain into a white elephant.

Inventory and equipment can be bought low, sold high

Again speaking of receiverships or business insolvencies, there are other items of interest which are frequently purchased by persons intimately familiar with their true values. One of these concerns inventories. Frequently, the merchandise is of salable character, and can be purchased for a fraction of cost. These items can be resold either to former customers of the insolvent, or to competitors which handle an identical grade or type of merchandise, or to surplus houses or jobbers. Sometimes this requires a little ingenuity and hard work, but the disposal is lucrative if the purchase price was right.

The second item is that of equipment and machinery. This is more difficult to move, except in times of war when equipment of any type is hard to secure. Usually, however, it can be bought at little more than junk value. It may be sold to small organizations using similar items, or it may be torn down and the parts sold separately—such as motors, fans, etc.

The third item is that of land and buildings. Usually these will bring only a fraction of book value. The buildings were probably constructed and arranged to meet the peculiar needs of that particular business, and others may be unable to visualize their conversion. Following the close of World War II, the properties owned by the government, or built with government funds, were frequently sold at figures around 10 per cent of their cost, yet they were suitable for conversion into other enterprises provided they could be handled in the areas in which those properties were then located.

Don't pay-off!

For example, following the close of World War II, the properties owned by the War Hemp administration were offered for sale. At the request of a couple of clients, I set up a proposed corporate structure to be called Midwest Feed Mills, Inc., which was for the purpose of converting them to alfalfa mills under new processing procedures then developed by these clients. After exhaustive months of work, and with considerable expert assistance, I set up a design for the structures, equipping them, handling their proposed operations, with cost figures, etc. Based on that, we approached underwriters and secured pledges of the necessary financial backing. At that point of time, my elbow was nudged and I was told that the proposition appeared so attractive that certain persons in the government wanted in for a share. At that point, I bowed out and washed my hands of the entire affair. It was my resolve then, and still is, that if I ever had to become engaged in any enterprise by paying off, in cash or otherwise, to government officials, I wanted no part of it.

It is essential, in any such situation, that considerable planning be done, with expert assistance. One must study the location of the structures, the proximity of roads and railroads, the amount of land under consideration, the construction and design of the buildings, the equipment available, and all other factors pertinent to any and all possible uses. The purchase must be based upon salvage prices; the resale must be based, after the new operations are complete and if a resale is made, upon the value of the property as a going business.

Check the accounts receivable

A fourth item is that of accounts receivable. Unless a receiver who is reasonably efficient is appointed, collections may be small and few. Some people make their entire business that of buying up accounts of defunct enterprises. During the period from 1930-1934, the accounts of defunct banks were sometimes bought as low as 2 per cent to 5 per cent on the dollar, yet collections were often made of 75 per cent to 80 per cent of those same accounts. In more normal times, this would not be the situation, but cash purchases will sometimes result in the acquisition of satisfactory receivables at a low rate.

The preceding discussion pertains to the separate pur-

chase of assets of a liquidated business. There are other possibilities which may be even better. Frequently, a business
is sound from the point of view of the product, production
methods, and sales demand but goes to the wall because of
incompetent or dishonest management. Or some other factor
may be involved which can be corrected under proper administration. After bankruptcy proceedings have started,
the creditors are the kings, acting through the trustee in
bankruptcy. However, they are unhappy monarchs. Not
only have they lost their accounts receivable, but they have
lost a customer.

Very frequently, then, a deal can be made where a sound
businessman steps in and arranges to purchase the business
intact for a fraction of its value as a going concern. He may
agree to take over the business upon a basis where he will
pay 25 per cent of all creditors' claims immediately, and an
additional 25 per cent in two years, to be repaid from earnings. The creditors charge off the remaining 50 per cent. If
bonds are outstanding, they may be treated as the claims of
other creditors, or upon a different basis. Stockholders' claims
are, of course, wiped out, since if those persons did not see
fit to advance additional funds to reorganize they have for-
feited all interest. Or, if stockholders want to retain an
interest, the entrepreneur may handle the details of reor-
ganization and put the corporation upon a sound basis in
return for a substantial percentage of the stock.

Look out for the unloader

But, mind you, I have stated "upon a sound basis." As I
point out elsewhere, it is not uncommon for persons to step
in and take a sick company, reorganize it, fire the skilled
personnel, curtail research and maintenance in order to show
a profit, boost the price of the stock, and then unload.

In the promotion of a corporation, some method is
usually devised of rewarding the entrepreneurs by an increase in the value of the stock. One method of financing

such a company would be as follows. The corporation would be organized for a total capitalization of $125,000. Of this amount, there would be 1,000 shares of $100 par preferred, each share having one vote. There would be 5,000 shares of $5 par common. Each purchaser of one share of preferred stock would be entitled to subscribe for two and one-half shares of common. The promoters would subscribe for the remaining $12,500 of common stock. Since the enhancement in value would be reflected solely in the common stock, if the corporation doubles in value the common stock would not merely double in value but in reflecting the added $125,000 it would increase six times in value. The reward for sound management would come through enhancing the value of the business. As a matter of fact, in view of our present high income taxes, it is impossible to attract competent management through a large salary alone. A capital gains rate is the only thing which remains reasonably attractive. The customary method, therefore, is to pay the new president or other officer a substantial salary and to give him a three to five year option to purchase a substantial number of shares of treasury stock. Then, if he doubles or triples corporate net income, the value of the treasury stock will rise proportionately; he can sell the options or purchase the stock, his tax being only upon the optional 25 per cent capital gains rate when the option stock is sold.

Of course, it is occasionally possible to interest management through the challenge afforded by a new or different business. Walter Chrysler acquired Delco solely for the purpose of getting Kettering. One man can be worth that. But even the acquisition of that corporation would not have brought Kettering to Chrysler had Chrysler not offered Kettering a challenge to which he responded.*

Corporations are often controlled through a comparatively small block of stock, and the tendency is to perpetuate management where it has been successful. In the case of

* *Life of an American Workman,* pp. 152-153.

major enterprises, where holdings are widely scattered, probably less than 10 per cent of the stock will be in the hands of any one person. The remaining persons normally fill in printed proxy cards which they receive through the mail and return them. They are thoroughly confused when a proxy fight develops, and they are solicited by several different groups of persons for such proxies. One of the most publicized fights in recent years was that staged by Louis Wolfson in Montgomery Ward & Company, where he felt certain changes in management policies were desirable. And, in situations such as that, frequently the decision of ultimate control may be tipped by banks which, acting as trustees or other legal representatives, hold sufficient of the stock to determine who shall constitute management. But banks are reluctant to exercise their discretion, because of the responsibility an erroneous decision may entail later.

Robert Young secured control of Chesapeake & Ohio, and allied enterprises, in the first instance by bucking the established order perpetuated through the proxy system. In his case, he emerged with desirable modifications of then existing railroad practices, and all railroads benefited thereby. Unfortunately, however, many persons stage proxy battles solely for the purpose of securing personal control of a corporation, or some element of domination over it; and such control is quite subject to abuse, in view of the stock option plans, pension plans, and high salaries which are usually put into effect when they have secured such control.

★   *Those situations, however, are normally for the affluent. At least, they are not situations with which most of us will ever come in contact. Therefore, more interesting to us are problems which arise in connection with the acquisition of the smaller business. The average situation here may involve a sole proprietorship, a partnership, or a family corporation. The business may be very sound and profitable, with an excellent*

*future, yet a purchase becomes possible. Why?
Generally for one of several reasons: (1) The key,
or an important officer or owner, dies; (2) A
divorce requires large ready cash or a splitting
of the business; (3) The persons in control of
management become old and want to retire; (4)
A disagreement between partners or key officers
arises and they decide to sell out.*

How to figure what a business is worth

Interestingly enough, even the best of such businesses
frequently can be bought at bargain prices. Assuming they
are soundly operated, with excellent future prospects, one
would follow a method of appraising value upon a minimum
basis. The land would be appraised as bare land, at current resale value, less 25 per cent for shrinkage. The buildings would carry replacement value, less depreciation upon
a schedule varying according to the type of construction—
and from this would be deducted the cost of immediate
necessary repairs. Machinery and equipment would be valued
midway between a low of salvage basis and a high of cost
less depreciation; inventories at cost; accounts receivable at
face minus charge-offs for obviously bad accounts and the
normal reserve for bad debts. Totalling these items would
give a basic, conservative value for resale.

Then the net annual earnings, prior to taxes, for the
preceding ten years would be analyzed. If it is apparent that
this figure is between 50 per cent and 100 per cent of the
basic figure above computed—and back orders and future
prospects are good—a purchase at the basic figure would be
an excellent one. Strangely enough, I have seen sales and
purchases at such figures repeatedly over recent years. No
person can afford to buy a business at a price which would
return only 10 per cent to 20 per cent prior to taxes. There
are too many uncertainties in business. Whether or not a
purchase should be made at 20 per cent to 50 per cent de-

pends upon how badly the buyer wants the business, and how much he can expand its operations. Over 50 per cent, any person should be able to make money, even after taxes are taken out.

Incorporate?

One who purchases a business upon such a basis often wants to recoup his purchase price rather quickly, particularly if he intends to buy other businesses. The quickest way is to incorporate it, take all of the stock, both preferred and common, sell his preferred stock bearing a five to six per cent return, perhaps at a discount to persons in the community (for whom it would be safe, as well as returning a reasonable interest), and then pay excellent dividends upon the common stock which he retains. He may then sell the common stock outright to an individual, to a group of individuals, or to a company engaged in a similar line of activity; or, if the corporation is large enough to be listed on an exchange, he may sell his common stock piecemeal. He may easily quadruple his investment—all upon a capital gains basis.

Referring again to Leopold Silberstein, he studied the holdings of Robert Young at a time when he knew that Mr. Young would be tied up in a terrific financial battle for control of the New York Central Railroad Company. He knew each item in the portfolio and the value thereof. One of the companies in which Mr. Silberstein wanted to become interested was Industrial Brownhoist. He also knew that that organization had a cash reserve of $13 a share. Therefore, when Robert Young needed all of the ready cash resources he could command, Mr. Silberstein purchased Industrial Brownhoist from him at exactly that $13 a share. A remarkable purchase, but the timing was perfect and the advance study was most careful.*

* *Operation Success*, p. 31.

The potential is the thing

There are men who make a living digging out such potential purchases of corporations and handling them upon a commission, or finder's fee, basis. However, a more lucrative field involves the ownership and control of the business. Even gigantic enterprises, such as Kruger & Toll, Insull, and others have been built upon the principle of acquiring enterprises and developing them, plus consolidation, and expansion. Ivar Kruger, for example, was once a streetcar conductor in Chicago. Back in his native Sweden, he became interested in the match industry and quickly rose to control of one such company. He worked out an amalgamation of competing companies, with himself at the head, and that was the foundation of his "match kingdom." Using the equity in one company to acquire another company, and so on, is the usual direction of growth, and such may lead to vast financial success. In this technique, however, there is also great danger. It is like buying stocks upon a narrow margin. When a squeeze comes, and a weak link snaps, the others may fall with it. In addition, in the United States, another danger of consolidation comes from the Sherman Anti-Trust Act and similar laws which might penalize the enterprise for stifling competition, require a separation of the businesses, or both. But, if the principles are used wisely, without jeopardizing financial security or violating anti-trust laws, the financial advantages to be gained are apparent.

Where the middleman makes money

A somewhat similar problem may arise in connection with large real estate holdings, particularly in connection with store or office buildings in cities, or lot locations for commercial building. Suppose John Jones finds that the Prudential Insurance Company wants to erect a ten-million dollar office building in Chicago, or a five-million dollar housing project in Peoria. In each case, let us say, there is only one ideal location. John Jones calls upon the owner of the property and dickers for an option to himself for such land. Then he turns around and deals with the Prudential. If Prudential had gone direct to the owner and disclosed its plans, the price would have skyrocketed. But it doesn't object to paying Jones a legitimate profit for his activity, and does so.

Or suppose the Commonwealth Title Company needs a larger building. The only one suitable without tremendous remodelling is the Acme Building. But the key men in each group detest each other. The potential buyer has no intention of even approaching Acme. But busy Johnny Jones, who has his ear to the ground, does go to Acme. Much to his surprise, Acme would like to sell and gives him an option. He deals with Commonwealth and secures a commitment upon a higher basis, which firm offer is placed in writing. Jones exercises his option, completes both contracts, and walks out with his profit. In other cases, Jones may take a share of stock in a building corporation in lieu of profit and receive a substantial income for the rest of his life from a single source.

These transactions are not at all uncommon. William Zeckendorf could give many instances of such transactions. Arnold Johnson, one-time owner of the Kansas City Athletics, was an expert in that field, and there are many others. Fred Saigh, former owner of the St. Louis Cardinals, laid the foundation for his wealth upon such a transaction.

If one intends to emulate these successful gentlemen, a good rule is—get it in writing. Many a man whose word is his bond becomes strangely absent-minded when there is no written agreement to refresh his recollection.

Critical time: When a business begins

A wholly different problem arises in connection with the establishment of a new enterprise. It must have a good product, production facilities, sales facilities, working capital, and management. Of these, management is by far the most important. The first question investment underwriters ask with reference to any new business is "Who is going to run it?" This requires not only men of integrity, but men with excellent backgrounds of successful management experience. The trouble with most persons who, perhaps, own a patent or a type of product offering good possibilities of development is that they fail to understand the financial and business problems involved. For example, bucking manufacturing costs when new dies, tools, machinery, etc., are required, when no assembly line procedures have yet been evolved, is rough as contrasted to a competing plant possessing the necessary techniques and equipment. It may be unprofitable to set up a manufacturing plant to produce a single item. It might be cheaper to subcontract the manufacture. Likewise, it may not be feasible to develop an individual sales force to sell a single item.

These, and many other problems, management is called upon to solve. Poor management means bankruptcy; good management may mean the development of a sound and growing enterprise. Therefore, anyone proposing to invest in a new corporation should regard it as a strictly speculative venture, being prepared to lose the money which he invests. He should never invest unless he is satisfied as to the possibilities of such enterprise from each point of view mentioned. And never, never should he advance his funds purely because of friendship for the promoter or investor. He had better spend it on wine, women, and song, instead. In the latter case, he will at least have pleasant memories.

PRACTICAL POINTERS

1. **You can use your money—sometimes even a small amount of money—to capitalize a business that needs money quickly. Under-capitalization causes**

many businesses to fail. Also it offers many opportunities for the investor when a capital-emergency
comes.

2. Good businesses often can be bought at bargain
prices. They may be sold even though they are
making money. But you must bring good management with you.

3. If it suits you, keep an eye on the business "bargain
counter." Get to be a judge of value; of buildings,
machinery, inventory and the like. Accounts receivable also are a great profit-item.

4. Big names are associated with buying-in, but the
more modest investor can follow the same principles.

5. Again, shoemaker stick to your last. The buying-in
process is good if you go at it in a professional manner, willing and able to assume the risk.

4

Real Estate Can Give You an Income—While Its Value Grows

MANY PEOPLE feel insecure with a bundle of gilt-edged securities but feel quite satisfied with the equivalent value in real estate. The reason is, I dare say, that real estate is something you can see, touch, walk on.

We have found out in the previous chapter, too, that real estate can be the only thing that retains value when an economy falls to pieces. After all, it is *real*.

So important is real estate as an investment—both in terms of income and in terms of "real" value—that I am going to devote several chapters to it. We'll look at many types of real estate, see what they have to offer and what their drawbacks may be.

We'll dabble in some of its problems—rents, upkeep, taxes, fair return—to give you an idea of when it's worthwhile to buy a building or a parcel; when to keep it; when to sell. We'll look at the process of buying and selling. And we'll see how American habits have made the motel a very attractive piece of real estate.

Just when is a piece of real estate a sound investment? This usually depends on the price paid for it, the income it will afford, and its possible resale. If you want to judge real estate in relation to the personal effort involved in taking care of it, I'd list it as follows in descending order of attractiveness: Industrial, commercial, residential. But there is no hard and fast rule.*

Where to find profitable real estate

How do you find such investments? There are many sources. First, it pays to have a friend who is a good, live wire real estate agent. Not only will he know of most good opportunities which come upon the market, but his judgment as to values will usually be sound. In addition, if the property is bought for resale, he can suggest the selling price and help to sell it. This, by all odds, is the best source of data.

The next most valuable source is classified newspaper advertising. One who makes a habit of studying these ads daily, over a period of years, and of inspecting representative properties will himself become quite expert in appraising their values and possibilities. Since many persons either list their properties personally, and have little conception of value, or have to make a sale in a limited period of time, occasionally a real bargain can be acquired. Any property which can be bought from between 25 per cent to 50 per cent less than current market upon similar property, and which is capable of quick resale, is regarded as a bargain property. No profit margin of less than 25 per cent will usually reimburse the investor for his expense, time, and trouble in purchase and resale.

* The excellent book by Nickerson, *How I Turned $1,000 into a Million in Real Estate—in my spare time*, 1959, Simon and Schuster, is a good text for the would-be investor in residential real estate.

A third source is through estates. If one living in a small county seat town keeps abreast of current estates either through the county or probate clerk's office, or through obituary notices, he can keep track of properties likely to come upon the market. If such properties are to be sold at private sale, he can ascertain the terms through the estate attorney and make a bid. If public sale is required, he may appear at the auction—never making a bid until it seems that other bidding has closed. If he starts bidding in the early stages, he may stimulate others; however, after most of the crowd has lost interest, a timely bid or two, with well spaced pauses in between, may well be successful.

Similarly, purchases may be made at receivership sales, master in chancery proceedings, bankruptcy sales, or tax sales. In all of these cases one should be familiar not only with the property but with the chain of title. No property should be bought unless the buyer is assured by his attorney that the title will not be subject to challenge.

The last method of finding possible purchases is by familiarizing one's self with particular properties, usually either rental or business properties, which are well located or valuable for some other purpose. The name of the owner can be ascertained through the tax records, title companies, or some official in the nature of a recorder of deeds—or simply by asking a knowledgeable person in that area. Occasionally such an owner is eager to sell; although where the approach is made by a prospective purchaser, the owner feels there is a keen interest in the property and his price tends to increase.

★   *Unless one is purchasing through a source where a single bid is all which can be submitted, he should generally not name his highest price during the first conference. It is always better to permit the seller to name his desired price—take some time to secure a few facts concerning needed repairs, tax rates, etc., and then to*

*counter with a lower offer. Usually the price will
wind up somewhere in the middle. However, this
will vary from one person to another, and is dependent upon competition from other purchasers.
One must vary his purchasing tactics according
to the situation.*

People who live in the particular community or in the
area seldom realize the opportunities available. They become
too accustomed to seeing a particular property upon the
market, or treat too lightly that which is in their vicinity.
By contrast, a stranger may readily see the values afforded.
A few years ago Raymond Collins (that is not his name)
moved from another city and bought a drugstore in the
community to which he moved. One year after he moved
there, he rented out upon a favorable monthly rental the
food and beverage portion of the store. That immediately
guaranteed him a definite income, with no headaches. He
then heard of a splendid apartment building property which
was for sale. The people who owned it were elderly, and
desired to move from the community. It had been financed
upon a long-term insurance company loan and could be
bought with almost no down payment. There were over
forty units in the building. He arranged to buy this property; then, when rentals were unfrozen, he was permitted
to adjust them upward. Finally, he rented upon a long
term basis the pharmaceutical portion of the drugstore to
a small chain. With the income derived from these three
sources, he promptly retired, and since then has enjoyed
touring South America, Europe, and the Caribbean. Those
opportunities were equally available to the people who were
long-time residents of the community; but they could not
see the opportunities present before their eyes.

Well-chosen words and a bucket of paint

After one has acquired property, his problem may be to lease or to sell it. He must learn the art of writing an interesting advertisement. One who skimps upon words, or who abbreviates them, leaves a poor impression upon the reader. Penny-pinching doesn't pay when you have something to sell. First, jot down notes upon the features which will be of particular interest to a buyer or tenant. Then these should be organized logically and interesingly, so that the reader can visualize the property. But it should not be exaggerated. The letdown to the one who comes to view the property will result in a loss of that prospect. If anything, a few features should be omitted from the advertisement but mentioned casually in showing the property.

Also, in selling real estate, it should be remembered that first impressions are lasting ones. A little paint, elbow grease, and good taste may wholly alter the appearance of a property. Let us say that one buys a house which was built in 1915. He pays $7,500 but wants to make a $4,000 profit. Often, there will be an old Chippendale style bathtub. This can be replaced at moderate expense and a modern tub installed. Imitation tile can be placed half-way up the bathroom walls and the upper walls painted. A woman then looks to the kitchen. Here, again, the sink and cabinets should be modern, the walls clean and sparkling. If the house has an old-fashioned parlor and sitting room, or even a dining room-parlor adjoining, but the parlor is small, the partition can be knocked out to form one huge room, which is redecorated. Upon the outside, clean paint (which should almost always be white with an attractive trim) will change the entire appearance. And, occasionally, an investment in landscaping will pay ample dividends. In the instance just given, an investment of $2,500 will often permit a sale of $14,000, which will yield the desired profit. This is only illustrative—as the same principles apply in any price range, except the top brackets, and they are poor investment properties, in all events. Frequently, a resale will be twice the amount of the purchase price, with only a small expenditure in renovation.

There are just a few other general principles which one should keep in mind with reference to all types of real estate. One should select tenants as carefully as possible. Whether a farm or an apartment is involved, one should seek persons who are good moral risks—who will not give cause for complaint to others nor cause undue damage to the property. This is a matter primarily of knowing people, and judging them by first impressions, although it is well to check references where feasible.

Hedge the risks

Next, one should always carry adequate insurance against all hazards. This involves primarily insurance against fire and extended coverages, public liability insurance including injuries and property damage to tenants, and workmen's compensation insurance if he has a janitor or other employees.

Third, one must evaluate the dangers of financial losses from causes beyond his control. This includes the possibility of a depression, with a resulting lessening of demand for rental properties, decrease in rentals, and decrease in values. One cannot always expect bonanza times. The possibility of war and its effect upon the community should be considered. Governmental restrictions upon rentals and upon resales are important factors affecting actual value to the owner.

Fourth, one should always reduce his agreements to writing, through a good attorney. Whether it be a contract of sale or a lease, misunderstanding and loss are avoided if the terms are in a written agreement not subject to the hazards of memory.

Fifth, properties should seldom be pyramided. In boom times, pyramiding may increase opportunities for profits, but in depressions it may mean the loss of all properties. Pyramiding results when one buys a piece of property, mortgages it to the hilt, uses the borrowed money to purchase another property, mortgages it, and so on. Few can afford to pyramid values except the man who has no need for this method of financing.

I know of one lady in our community who was left a widow with several young children who became wealthy by pyramiding property purchases in the 1920's. I know of two elderly bachelors who also built up a tremendous number of properties the same way in the two decades before 1930; but who lost about 60 per cent of their properties during the first three years of the depression by reason of the inability to meet mortgage payments when practically all rental income suddenly ceased. But this caution does not prevent wisely planned exchanges of smaller for larger properties, as one increases his equities.

Have you a real estate temperament?

There is no question but that excellent money can be made in rental real estate, and there is a permanence about the investment which makes it attractive. It is not a situation of buying a piece of paper and seeing it suddenly become valueless. There are attractive income tax advantages, in that the depreciation schedules permit one to accumulate funds for the acquisition of other property, for the retirement of obligations, for the creation of capital gains, or for the purpose of simply spending it. On the other hand, there are headaches connected with rental property—such as in the payment of taxes and special assessments, repairs, occasional rental losses, advertising for new tenants, showing of the property, replacing of furniture in the case of furnished apartments, etc. Unless one is sufficiently placid of temperament to endure such minor troubles with equanimity, rental property is not his type of investment.

Income taxes upon real estate

In view of the fact that income taxes are such an important aspect of property ownership, let us discuss them in more detail. In the case of either new or old construction, this income tax advantage exists. Even though the owner maintains the property in top shape, so that its value may increase yearly, and even though he may charge off such repairs as expenses from his income for tax purposes, he has the advantage of a depreciation schedule. This means that he may set a building up on a 20 to 50 year schedule, varying as its age and construction vary, and personal property upon an average of a 10 year basis, and by these deductions reduce his taxable income. To illustrate this more specifically, let us take a frame 6-apartment building for which the owner pays $25,000 and installs $5,000 of furniture and equipment. Of the $25,000 investment, $5,000 is included in a furnace, hot water heater, and other fixtures which are estimated at a life of 15 years. The owner receives a gross income per year of $7,500 and has expenses for utilities, taxes, repairs, insurance, heat, etc., of $2,500. Let us figure, briefly, his taxable income.

The net annual income, prior to depreciation, is $7,500 less $2,500 or $5,000. Now let us see how important depreciation is. After deducting fixtures, a base of $20,000 is left for the building which, on a 25 year basis, permits him to deduct $800 from income. The furniture, being upon a 10 year basis, permits him to deduct an additional $500 per year. The fixtures, being upon a 15 year basis, permits him to deduct an additional $333.33 per year. Adding these items together, we obtain a deduction of $1,633.33, so that the owner pays income tax only upon $3,366.67, instead of upon $5,000.

Now this is not all gravy. The deduction of depreciation reduces the base cost of the property, thereby increasing the gain upon a resale. But this may be computed upon the

favorable capital gains rate, which never exceeds half the
regular income tax rate. So the institution of depreciation is
blessed by those who own buildings for investment purposes.

Trading up

Even more desirable than paying income taxes at capital
gains rates is the prospect of paying no income taxes at all,
or at least deferring them indefinitely so that one's maximum
capital can always be at work. And this can be done. There
is an exemption from taxes upon property exchanges of
"like for like," except as to "boot" received in such an
exchange.

In simple terms, if you swap rental property for rental
property, receiving no cash for the value of any part of
your interest, there is no tax then payable. The whole thing
becomes a bookkeeping transaction with an accounting to
be made when the properties ultimately are converted into
cash.

So you start with a $10,000 property, let us say, and
improve it and reduce its mortgage until you have a net
equity of $8,000. You may then swap for a run-down prop-
erty then worth $20,000 minus a mortgage of $12,000. By
improving it and paying down its mortgage, it may be
exchanged for a still more valuable property, potentially,
and so on.

Many people want to trade larger properties for smaller
because of: (1) the expense, or work, of reconditioning the
larger property; (2) to reduce management responsibilities;
(3) smaller properties are more easily converted to cash. But
you, who are blessed with energy but want to build up your
assets, prefer to climb the ladder, rather than to descend it.

Build or buy?

In considering the desirability of building versus purchasing existing structures, much depends upon the situation of

the individual. If rents are frozen solidly upon older structures, and there are no rent controls upon new buildings,
the latter are generally preferred. If credit restrictions are
stringent upon old properties, but extremely liberal upon
new, a small equity payment may purchase a much better
new property than old. If one is a contractor, or can procure
all materials at cost, or if building costs are in a trough,
new construction may be preferred. However, when materials are scarce, labor costs are high and all credit restricted,
it is almost always more profitable to purchase existing
structures. One must then, however, take into consideration
expenses which may be incurred in modernizing such buildings, as well as the great expense in upkeep and maintenance.
One invariable rule which I follow is to have a competent
contractor go with me through every proposed purchase,
inspecting the foundation, exterior, interior, woodwork, furnaces, boilers, wiring, piping, plumbing, roofs, ceilings, and
all other structural portions. Such an inspection will knock
many deals in the head, but will save untold grief and
expense.

Large or small?

If one considers the acquisition of houses, he should give
some thought to the type of dwelling which he wants to
own. As income property, large, well-built, expensive homes
are strictly white elephants. Suppose one figures merely
upon a 10 per cent gross return upon his investment. Five
per cent may pay his taxes, repairs, and upkeep—but it will
not provide for depreciation. And how many tenants would
be willing to pay, let us say, 10 per cent of $35,000 as an
annual rental? This would be approximately $300 a month.

As a consistent, small yield investment, which is also
capable of resale, the two or three bedroom house, in an
area of small, comparatively new homes, in a respectable
section of town, close to schools, parks, and bus lines is the
best housing investment for combining security and income.

Attractiveness of the interior and exterior helps to increase rentability and salability of such property. One should always figure here on a 15 per cent gross annual return based upon purchase price.

From the point of view of income alone, often the very poorest type of housing returns the best income over a period of many years. It is unfortunate that persons often acquire such property who have no pity for those who occupy them. This situation is being somewhat corrected with the increase in public housing, but there still remains many slum areas. Yet I have seen people make excellent incomes from such property, charging modest rentals, by permitting the tenants to cooperate in the upkeep of the property. Since those persons who occupy them are often handy with their hands, the owner normally furnishes the lumber and other materials necessary for repairs or remodelling of the property, including paint, and charges a reduced rental by giving credit for the improvement performed upon the property. In that way, the property can be put into excellent condition, kept in good repair, and remain rented consistently. Here, however, the matter of the selection of good tenants is all important, and unless one owns a number of such properties, such an investment will entail more of a gamble than it is worth.

The duplex

One of the better investments is the well designed duplex. Persons who like the convenience of an apartment and the privacy of a home find a duplex the perfect solution—particularly the modern ranch style, where both units are upon the first floor. With modern heating and plumbing units, small duplexes with one or two bedrooms, and a combined utility and furnace room, can be attractively designed and soundly constructed at a fairly moderate cost. Here, the gross annual return should range between 15 per cent and

20 per cent of construction cost, so that even in depression periods the owner will still earn interest upon his money.

The individual units in a duplex usually should be unfurnished. Persons who have reached the duplex stage almost always have furniture of their own. Also, furniture upkeep expense far exceeds the cost of structural maintenance. As high a rental can be secured for an unfurnished, as for a furnished, unit because of the demand for such properties. Occasionally, stoves and refrigerators are furnished, but these are long-lived and do not greatly increase the average overhead.

One advantage of a duplex over apartment properties is that the owner need not have a janitor to furnish heat, cut grass, or do like work. That is the task of the tenants, even as in a private home. This, also, reduces overhead materially.

Such duplexes should be well located, following the tests previously discussed for the erection of private homes for resale. If they are, and are attractively designed, resale is no great problem.

In connection with any type of rental property, of course, the possibility of rent controls must be considered. Such controls necessarily operate with great unfairness in a period of rising costs. The net revenue to the landlord decreases as taxes, labor costs, repairs, equipment, and material increase in price—yet his rentals remain constant. Wages rise as do farm prices and the cost of retail goods; he alone is penalized. Therefore, one must be willing to risk such discrimination if he acquires property for rental. Upon the investment side, a few years ago, the very fact of such rent controls depressed the value of certain properties frozen at unusually low ceilings and made them attractive purchases, bearing in mind the ultimate removal of controls. Their value did not keep pace with the inflationary trend of other investments.

Money in old houses

There are many new apartment buildings now being built to partially solve the housing problems in metropolitan areas and moderate sized communities. Where this is done upon a standardized pattern, such a venture may give a fair return for the investment. From a point of view of rental return alone, rather than stability of investment, the best buys are frequently the mammoth old houses which have been converted into from 6 to 18 apartments of varying sizes. These may occasionally be bought at a figure which will return 25 per cent to 35 per cent annual gross upon the investment. At least, this is true if the landlord does not put too much back into redecorating and new furniture. My own trouble is in being softhearted, and in looking at an apartment from the tenants' point of view. My tenants may love me, but, actually, it's probably not good business.

However, converted apartments which are not attractively maintained are of the marginal variety. In depression times, when families double up—or in building booms when houses are more plentiful—they are the first to be vacated, the first upon which rents must be cut sharply. Still, however, if rented at only half of top rentals, the gross return should be sufficient to allow a satisfactory depreciation program and to allow a reasonable interest return. If the location is close to a business area, the property may become even more valuable for commercial usage.

The trend is, of course, to garden type apartments, or so-called ranch style—where all apartments are on the first floor, with ample yard and recreational facilities. Since these are still practically non-existent, they are not available except by building them, which often is not economically feasible. This does mean, however, that the three- or four-floor walk-up type of apartment will depreciate in value in future years when opposed by such competition. One must realize the future detriments to any type of investment property.

Walk-ups; a good buy

Considering elements of security, long term return, and peace of mind, the best buys in the apartment field are two-story, walk-up types, brick or stone buildings, situated in a comparatively new area of attractive, moderate sized homes. If they are situated in an area of large homes, while these may be more flashy in the beginning, such areas deteriorate more rapidly. This is true for several reasons. The smaller homes cannot be converted into competing apartments; the large ones can be. The larger homes have a high resale price which few persons can or will pay. The only method of the owner recouping his cost is by conversion into smaller housing units, or, in short, apartments. These generally go from good, to bad, to worse; whereas the individual home owners tend to maintain their houses and their yards in a rather uniform manner.

There being no elevators to operate in a walk-up apartment, upkeep and repairs upon elevators are eliminated as well as the expense of an operator. Many older persons dislike the self-operated type of conveyance. One of the tenants can receive a rental rebate for maintenance of the premises and cleaning the halls and sidewalks, leaving little to trouble the owner.

Before purchasing such properties, the same type of inspection should be made by a contractor as has been recommended for other properties. One should know exactly what expense must be anticipated in his first five to ten years of ownership. The gross return of any investment means nothing unless a net profit will result, in good times and bad. It's the net return which really matters. And marginal buys are bad investments. But if the property is sound and so priced that the purchaser can expect not less than a 15 or 20 per cent gross annual return upon his investment, taking vacant periods and depression rentals into consideration, the purchase usually is a sound one. To find such properties, one should make a survey of all possible structures in the area in which he is interested and keep current with changes in the financial positions and mental attitudes of their owners. He may also study the classified ads, keep in touch with leading realtors, and perhaps in touch with the settlement of estates, where heirs are scattered and the property must be liquidated for distribution or for the payment of estate tax claims.

One of the popular methods of selling apartment buildings, in order to derive the maximum gain, is by selling it piecemeal. This is usually done by forming a corporation and selling stock in it to the tenants, which purchase carries with it the ownership of one of the apartments; or by selling interests in the real estate itself, as in a condominium, where state law permits. Generally these are cooperative types of ventures, the tenants or owners thereafter dividing maintenance expenses among themselves in proportion to the size of the apartments.

Money in rooming houses

Few persons think of rooming houses as an investment, except for widows or others living in college towns who take in students to help defray expenses. Actually, such a property can be a fair revenue producer. If the building is large enough to have 12 or more rental rooms above the first floor, exclusive of a sitting room for the students, the first floor can be turned over rent free to a couple which is engaged to maintain the premises, keep order, and clean the upstairs. At going rates, they would probably receive $50 a month, in addition to free rent. Utilities and repairs would run an average of $125 a month additional, for an annual expenditure of $2,100 exclusive of taxes and insurance. With a going rental rate of approximately $40 per room (based upon a year around rate) the gross annual income would be in excess of $5,700, leaving a net of approximately $3,000. Since such large barns of places can frequently be bought for a price of between $20,000 and $30,000, the net income return is not unattractive. Boarding houses, on the other hand, are absolutely *verboten* for an absentee landlord.

Look into motels

Tourist homes are flatly out as a possible source of revenue, except for a couple desiring to supplement a small income by use of a few rooms in their own home. Tourist courts, motels, and motor inns are a different proposition— and these are now being scrutinized carefully by excellent investors as the logical successors to hotels. Except in large metropolitan areas, or for the convenience of persons travelling without an automobile, hotels can no longer compete with first-class motels. The convenience of having one's car within touching distance, instead of in a garage two blocks away, the safety of modern construction, the economies resulting from the elimination of storage bills, numerous tips, and petty charges all are conducive to a favorable nod toward the motor courts.

No motel containing less than twelve units can be profitable, except where owner-operated. The initial managerial expense would consume the profit, coupled with general overhead and employees' salaries. Assuming that the area in question will support an unlimited number of units, the larger the number of units, the more profitable will be the operation. One can use a smaller number of regular employees in proportion to the structures, achieve economies in operation and in the purchases of supplies and equipment, and attract better management.

The location counts

In any community, the location of such motels is important. They should be upon the most travelled highway and not too remote from the next busiest road. They should not be in an area surrounded by shacks or unattractive structures. Preferably they should be built well back from the highway and attractively landscaped. Under no circumstances should they be close to a noisy railroad or to manufacturing plants. Insofar as possible, the style of architecture should conform to the section of the country where located. And the best investments a motel can make are in the excellence of its mattresses and soundproofing of its rooms.

If one is either planning to construct a motel, or to purchase a going business, he would do well to consider the climatic and geographical factors. For example, New England is largely an area of home owners. The natives do little travelling where they patronize motels. The tourists do all of their visiting during a very few months. Therefore, one's annual revenue is limited largely to such periods. Almost any area having a very cold climate during fall and winter months is subject to like objections.

Similarly, those southern states which have extremely hot summers have few travellers during those months. Southern Arizona would be an example of this. Of course, the revenue may be sufficient during a few months to compensate for inactivity the remainder of the year.

What makes people sleep over?

As a general rule, the hotels in moderate sized communities are not of plush character, so as to create unbeatable competition. This is one reason to locate at the edge of a smaller town. Again, the tourist in such an area may stay at a motel without being inconvenienced by a long drive to the business section. Yet, there must be reasons for people to stop there overnight—either because it is the logical break upon a long trip, or because the surrounding country and the community are so attractive as to induce them to remain. There may be business or other motives—such as Las Vegas and Reno, with their divorce and marriage mills, and with their gambling.

While it is impossible to lay down unalterable rules, except in metropolitan centers, it does seem evident that, by and large, motels will, in future years, profit more south of the Mason-Dixon line than north of it—and particularly in certain areas of Florida, parts of Texas, Tennessee, the

Gulf coast, and also in California. In more typical resort country, such motels can be expanded into vacation resorts with only moderate structural changes, but with greatly increased revenue.*

The motel-resort

In discussing resorts, one should bear in mind, in considering either summer or winter resorts, that there are vast differences in the caliber of various places. An ultra-swank resort takes in a much larger revenue per diem—it also has a much larger basic cost, an expanded overhead, and many headaches. Since there are many more middle-class people than persons of wealth, the demand is much greater for moderate-priced, family-type resorts which do not furnish all recreational facilities, but where recreational facilities are readily accessible.

The ideal situation is to have a place which is fundamentally a motel, but sufficiently attractive to double as a resort, inducing overnight guests to remain for several weeks. If, for example, one has a spot of this character, attractively landscaped, along the southern part of either coast of Florida, he would need only two things to transform it into an attractive resort. One is a well designed small swimming pool. The second is a restaurant serving excellent food. The location should be so selected that golf courses, deep-sea fishing, and riding facilities are not too remote—and arrangements can be made for the guests for such entertainments. One can, then, handle both tourist and resort grade with equal ease.

It is necessary, in making any investment, to peer somewhat into the future. It is not too difficult to appreciate which areas in the country are receiving the largest proportion of population growth, nor to predict the directions and tendencies of tourist travel. If these factors are kept in

* See the excellent discussion in "Luxury Hotels Along the Highway," *Coronet*, May, 1959, p. 32.

mind, one may avoid buying into some venture which has no present volume of desirable business nor any great hope for the future. And while the best motel in an area may be an excellent investment, a marginal venture may develop quickly into a place of business for ladies of easy virtue. It costs even more to maintain poor construction than well-built structures. Accordingly, in investing in existing businesses of this type, stay away from second raters—look only at the best, places which you would count yourself lucky to find, if travelling.

PRACTICAL POINTERS

1. Real estate investments have much to offer because:
    A. They are permanent.
    B. They produce income in most cases.
    C. They can appreciate in value.
    D. They give you a tax advantage.
    E. They help you hedge against inflation.
    F. They offer broad opportunity for the investor, with many good deals often "right under your nose."
2. There are many different kinds of buildings, used for many different purposes. Know about them. Judge them in relation to their surroundings, business conditions and what you can tell of the future. (Just like any other investment.)
3. Rental properties should return at least 10% net per year. Sometimes the worst-looking properties are the best income producers, but they have other disadvantages.
4. Buying and selling real estate is an art in itself. Learn the rules.
5. The latest big producer in real estate is the motel. Especially for the owner-manager, it can be a very good thing.

5

Real Estate: Look Ahead
When You Deal in
Business Property

WE HAVE DISCUSSED the opportunities and hazards in residential types of real estate. Less well-known to the average investor, but often very profitable, is ownership of commercial real property.

Such an investment requires a good deal of business knowledge and also some imagination, for with business property it is especially important to look far ahead.

In this chapter we'll consider the opportunities in buying or leasing stores, factory sites and factories, shopping centers, office buildings and the like. We'll take a trip to the outskirts of town, too, and see how money is made—and lost—in subdividing farm land. Since even a ninety-nine-year lease comes to an end, we'll look into reversionary interests.

For hundreds of years there was little change in building methods. As a result, with materials and labor costs rising higher and higher, it has become too expensive to mark each piece of lumber on the job, cut by hand and throw the wastage away. We have seen the birth of prefabricated and pre-cut homes, of concrete-shell construction and other techniques that give the occupant of realty more for his money.

Wherever we are approached for investments, either upon building bonds or common stock, we should measure the structure by certain tests. Does the particular building have permanent beauty, utility, and value? Will it continue to enhance in value, or will it become obsolescent rapidly? These are certainly things which we should consider before risking our dollars.

Take a long, hard look around

Frequently, we may have an opportunity to purchase an old building, or an interest in an older structure. In such a situation, it is most important to recall the necessity of a thorough study by an expert contractor of that particular building. For example, about ten years ago a friend of mine became intrigued by a building which occupied some trackage space in Chicago, and housed primarily a number of light manufacturing industries. He sent me certain information which had been furnished by the seller, which showed a gross income of 25 per cent to 30 per cent, a sound location, and a well designed structure. I went to Chicago to look at the building.

As we entered the building, we found there were only two freight elevators to serve some eighteen separate businesses. We found the interior floors to be springy by jumping upon them, indicating an inability to hold a heavy load with safety over a period of time. Checking later with tenants, we found the building had been condemned by the fire authorities in the absence of extension structural supporting, plus new exits and fire escapes. One can often learn from tenants the nature of any problems existing. Going back to the inspection, the corridors were winding; the floors and halls bore no indications of paint or varnish; the stairs sagged. The brick walls were old, badly in need of pointing up; the roof was old and defective. Only one loading dock existed for the use of all these businesses.

It was apparent that necessary repairs and remodelling would greatly exceed the original cost. Since my friend was still undecided, I took him to one of the larger banks in Chicago and contacted one of the vice-presidents. He made a few inquiries around his office and located a file involving this property. It showed that the property had been purchased under a foreclosure sale some ten years before at one-fourth the present asking price. The banker then made a few more inquiries as to the present seller, and within an hour's time we had a credit history upon him which showed clearly that any statement by him should be regarded with great skepticism. Needless to say, the deal was abandoned.

An even more careful inspection and analysis would have been in order if this deal had approached the negotiation stage. The furnaces, boilers, plumbing, structure, and all other features would have been checked in detail; the leases, duration, terms, rental figures, and financial worth of tenants would have been examined; estimates from reliable contractors as to remodelling would have been necessary.

This does not mean that light manufacturing locations are not sound. A well-constructed building, occupied by good tenants upon long term leases, is an excellent ownership proposition. But the structure must be well located, with adequate trackage space and loading docks, facilities to handle the requirements of all tenants, and it must be in sound condition.

Look around downtown

Business locations in a downtown area may be sound investments, generally increasing in value as time goes on. While it is true that business areas tend to decentralize, in favor of areas having adequate parking space, nevertheless the concentrated shopping centers do not normally diminish in value. As a simple suggestion to those who contemplate purchasing such business sites, I propose this for their consideration. The first floor area can be rented, together with the basement, to a sound tenant—frequently a chain clothing store—for a ten year period at a total sum sufficient to capitalize the entire investment, with the tenant required to pay real estate taxes and to keep the property in sound repair. A loan can be made at a low interest rate, secured by the lease, for the majority, or sometimes even all, of the purchase price. The second and third floors may be rented to other tenants. Or, if the tenant takes over the entire building, a higher rental often may be secured.

Such locations may, for a building 40' x 100', bring rentals from $200 to $2,000 a month in even modest-sized communities, dependent on the type of structure, its use and its location.

Of course, the owner will have to pay income taxes upon the rentals received. He may also be required to regard as income the payments made by the tenant to preserve the structural portions of the property, and perhaps other items. However, he can depreciate the structure and the improvements. And, if he is in a high personal income tax bracket, he can form a building corporation to own and to manage the property which will pay at a lower tax rate. At the end of his ten year period, by sacrificing income tax payments, he will have acquired a sound property which he can keep for income or sell at the favorable capital gains tax rate.

Shopping centers are big business

A contractor who owns a subdivision will often hold out a tract for a neighborhood shopping center having adequate parking space—with the buildings constructed according to a consistent, attractive form of architecture. It is often not necessary for the owner personally to build a building. Frequently he can secure a deal with a grocery chain, oil company, or others to construct the building, pay a low lease price for a twenty year period plus taxes and maintenance of the building for the term of the lease, with the building becoming the property of the owner at the end of that time. If an option to renew the lease is reserved, it will be for a much higher rental.

In view of the attractiveness of such deals, it behooves an investor to anticipate the direction of city growth, to select areas which will be of particular value as shopping centers or for business locations, and to acquire them. Instead of sitting on his haunches, however, waiting for lessees to find him, he should visualize the possibilities of the location, contact persons who might be interested, and sell them upon the site.

It is normally considered that a regional shopping center must draw from a population area of not less than 225,000 people, living within a radius normally of five miles—although there are situations where such a center may draw from fifteen miles or even further. However, that is unusual. In such event, the regional shopping center must have access to major highways radiating in at least two and preferably four directions. If it is the hub of a series of spokes extending outwards, its prospects are good. However, the promoters of shopping centers often make a mistake by hurrying to get their initial tenants. In doing so, they frequently make deals with the type of a chain store operation which discourages others, and better, tenants from entering such location; and often the more favorable rentals which are given to these first tenants prevent charging more adequate rentals later on.

There is a marked future at the present time for both regional and neighborhood shopping centers. Whereas at one time the common plan for such developments was to have parking space beside each store, the accepted plan is to have perimeter parking, which means that the parking extends completely around the outside and the stores are huddled adjacent to each other, so that the woman shopper may walk easily from one to the next. I have often wondered why such shopping centers are not operated in conjunction with open-air theaters utilizing, to some extent in common, certain of the parking facilities, in view of the fact that they are not competitive, by and large, for the space at the same hours of the day and night.

How to make money by waiting

Of course, it is not always necessary to build something, or to buy a building, in order to make money from real estate. Not long ago, a prominent real estate man said, "If I had $20,000 I didn't need right now, I'd buy land on the highway a mile or so out of town, and then let the town grow to meet me. I would double my money in five years." A man in Bloomington, Illinois, did just that—except that he quintupled his money in approximately the same length of time. My wife's grandparents never had much money. But when her grandfather retired, they moved to Los Angeles, at which point his wife took over the handling of the funds. She would buy some property on the outskirts of Los Angeles, and within a very few years it would double its value. She would sell it and buy some property a little further out, and so on. She had a native shrewdness when it came to dealing with property. As a result, the old folks lived comfortably during their retirement years and left modestly substantial sums to each of their two boys.

Ins and outs of subdivision

This is all well and good when one deals with vacant property, buying it and selling it as such, without a great deal of investment being required in order to make it salable. However, people dream of the many thousands of dollars to be made from subdivisions. They dream of buying farm land for $500 an acre, cutting each acre into five lots, and selling each lot for $1,500 to $3,000. There are a few drawbacks to this plan. The dreamer forgets, for example, that the minute he subdivides land, the faithful assessor is waiting to swoop upward the value of such land upon the tax books. Also, before people will build, they need certain things. Water, gas, and electricity usually can be secured by making deposits, which may be repaid. But perhaps the water lines may require extension 800 to 1,000 feet to get to the subdivision. The cost of this must be paid.

More costly, however, are the items of street pavement, curb and gutter, sidewalk, sanitary sewer, storm sewer, and street lights. At the present time concrete pavement averages about $10.50 a square yard, sidewalks, curb, and gutter $4.25 a running foot combined, storm sewer (not including the cost of interceptor connections) $2.95 a running foot, sanitary sewer $1.80 a foot, and modern street lights approximately $4.25 a foot. These costs will vary, of course, depending upon labor costs in the geographical area, size of tile, quality of construction, and like items. But, assuming a street 30 feet in width, the cost of these improvements alone, excluding gas and water, will run $2,372.50 for a 75 foot lot—not counting cost to the owner at street junctions, side street improvements, and the like. And, as it takes quite a while to sell all lots, the investor has a considerable loss of interest upon the invested funds. Of course, he must also pay brokerage commissions upon lot sales, if he wants to move them expeditiously, which cost will probably run another $100 to $200 per lot minimum.

Profit can evaporate

I have seen subdivisions which would gross $80,000 in lot sales, where the owners had invested over $100,000 in taxes and special assessments alone—wholly forgetting the original cost of acquisition and loss of interest. Money has been made in subdivisions, of course, but they are rare instances and were handled with skill and dispatch.

The only way in which money can be made from subdivisions is to (1) hold the improvements to a minimum; (2)
keep the lots small; (3) sell them at reasonable prices; (4) get
rid of them fast. Street lights and sidewalks can be omitted
during the developmental stages. Asphalt can be used in place
of concrete. These factors would cut the improvement cost
in half. Then the owner must either cooperate with a contractor who takes over the entire tract and develops it
rapidly, or he must get several houses started in the area and
promote the daylights out of the rest of the lots. One entering this field for speculation must bear these factors in mind:
(1) How rapidly is the town growing? (2) What is the
extent of its housing shortage? (3) What is the natural
direction of desirable residential growth? He must also put
reasonable building restrictions in the area so that a lot buyer
has no fear as to the type of structure which will be built
next to him.

The gold along the railroad tracks

Far better than these nice, clean subdivisions is the nice,
dirty, smoky vacant land by railroad tracks. The reason is
apparent. Commercial and industrial locations are far more
valuable than residential sites. They are also more limited.
Under most zoning laws, industrial plants may be erected
in only one or two locations. They all need trackage space,
and many of them also need access to highways for truck
shipments. The ideal, the perfect, spot would be a large
island bounded on two sides by the main railroads running
north and south, and east and west, with the other two
boundaries formed by main highways paralleling the railroads. Of course, the ideal is seldom found—but often ample
trackage space can be bought at a bargain price. Then one
can either use a lease method, as described previously, or
develop interest in such tract from the point of view of sale.

The best of such sites would be in towns larger than
100,000 population—towns booming industrially, with every

reason for continued expansion. Denver, for example, with power and water facilities, would be a proper type of community. Peoria would be another. Right now, New Orleans and Baton Rouge are the hottest regions of development in the entire nation, from an industrial point of view—for many reasons, ample water (which is one of the most important items in industrial work), warm climate, inexpensive shipping, access from water, land, and air, and other advantages. I predict that similar industrial expansion may be expected in other sizable water-front communities possessing similar advantages. And, by the way, land which would not bring $10 an acre a few years ago is bringing as much as $5,000 an acre in the New Orleans-Baton Rouge development at the present time.

And wipe the windshield

Many investors are finding good business opportunities in sites for filling stations. Here, again, the ownership of land is required to be upon a busy highway, often at the outskirts of town, or at the intersection of two busy highways. In that event, the oil company generally builds its building, which eventually becomes the property of the land owner, and pays an adequate rental. It is a most satisfactory type of property ownership.

Of course, there is always the chap who held a piece of vacant land for twenty years, paying taxes on it all that time, only to have the town grow in a different direction and leave him stranded out among the hoot-owls. But this man should have been able to observe, over the years, what was happening to the community. He should have sold long before those twenty years went by.

★   *In real estate as in securities, the principle is the same: A bad investment should be cut loose even at a loss, and the money then wisely reinvested to build up the shrunken capital. Don't be*

sentimental about investments that turn sour—
get rid of them, and profit at least by your
experience.

In the case above, the real loss was not as great as the apparent loss. It should be borne in mind that the owner had the benefit of income tax deductions for real estate taxes and interest on his mortgage, if any. Nor did he pay income tax on dividends he might have realized if the money had been otherwise invested. These things should be taken into account, although they are a rather cold comfort.

Drawbacks in office buildings

A type of business rental property which I personally do not like too well is the office building. Unless such a building can be purchased at an unusually low price, or has intrinsic value because of the first floor locations for store purposes, it usually is not as attractive as other investments. Some reasons are: (1) Taxes are high; (2) Such a building usually requires recurrent outlays in repairs, remodelling, repainting, etc.; (3) Overhead is high because of utilities, salaries of janitors, elevator operators, and other employees; (4) An office building has a comparatively short period of existence prior to obsolescence; (5) In depression periods, tenants are hard to attract and rentals are low. Long term leases do not furnish the same degree of protection which they provide upon commercial properties.

Office buildings, therefore, present a lower proportionate income return, greater outlays for expenses, and less security than other business properties. Except for insurance companies, which can be satisfied with a moderately low net income return, they will not often prove desirable.

Reversionary interests

To be considered also are the possibilities inherent in buying reversionary interests in existing long term leases. Fifty or sixty years ago, many persons made ninety-nine year leases upon valuable commercial properties. As a general rule, their heirs value the interest which they retain at almost nothing, if the entire consideration was paid at the inception of the lease, or figure it at the capitalized rental value if an annual payment is received. As these leases draw closer to expiration dates, the reversion becomes increasingly more valuable. Careful searching of the records in metropolitan areas will often disclose such possibilities. The titles to the properties must be completely analyzed, and the interests of all parties in interest—or at least some of them —purchased. If the reversion may terminate beyond one's own normal life expectancy, it may be acquired in the name of a trustee for the benefit of one's children and prove to be a valuable inheritance.

Some persons I know make a practice of purchasing the interests of heirs in an estate. Frequently, heirs are hard-pressed financially or unwilling to wait the period of the estate proceedings for their inheritances. While these purchases may prove to be excellent bargains, they are extremely speculative. A will may be set aside, a new will discovered, or unexpected claims may consume an entire estate. It may be well to acquire reversionary interests, as mentioned, from heirs; but, ordinarily, the purchase of the more ordinary expectancies has serious hazards.

Technique of the lease-back

One of the more modern methods of financing the acquisition of business properties is the technique known as the sale and lease-back. This is a technique whereby one purchases a property and then turns around and leases it back to the same organization from which he purchased it. The reason is simply that the seller often needs cash, or at least needs to reduce the frozen assets in its portfolio; also, because the seller feels it can secure a more favorable income tax position by paying annual rentals than by depreciating its own building. It may even have depreciated the building down to the point where it cannot secure a favorable income tax position, and can sell the building for purposes of capital gains. In those situations, such a seller is often willing to accept a lower price than would ordinarily be the situation upon the commercial market.

It is not unusual, in such a transaction, for the seller of the property to take back a lease for a sufficient length of time to guarantee that the payments upon the purchase price will be met. Where this is the situation, the entire transaction can frequently be financed through an insurance company loan. Accordingly, the buyer can for little or no cash money acquire ownership of a property which is leased back to the seller; and, while his net income during the period of the purchase may be small, his net worth is substantially enhanced by the value of the reversionary interest in the property.

There are tax consequences to be considered in such situations which, however, require the consultation of an expert tax attorney. Of course, wherever a situation of that magnitude is involved, it is clear that one is going to have an attorney to assist him in the matter. He should be sure to associate a competent tax attorney, as well.

PRACTICAL POINTERS

1. **Buy commercial real estate with an eye to the future.**
2. **Never buy an existing building until a competent contractor gives his okay.**
3. **Well-located store buildings, bought at a proper**

price, are excellent investments; office buildings usually are not.

4. Vacant industrial locations may offer the greatest possibilities for profit.

5. With today's motorized population, the shopping center with ample parking space can give a high return.

6. The lease-back system often works well. Here, as elsewhere, keep your eye on tax savings.

6

Where Good Management
Makes Good Money

UP TO NOW we have emphasized the ways you can invest your money. But in talking about the stock market, real estate, business enterprise and so forth, we must not forget that most people first have to earn money to invest.

With the philosophy of investment fairly well hammered down, then, let us go on into fields of earning. We'll start with enterprises that generally put a man in business for himself. As you will see, there is often not much difference between earning money by actual work and earning money by letting your money work.

We'll see how some enterprising people have turned their hobbies into good business; how the wholesaler and jobber operate; and what kind of money the small retailer can expect to make.

Then we'll have a detailed look at the restaurant business—an enormous field with many levels; and we'll look into contracting, or the business of doing the actual work that puts roofs over people's heads.

I hope you'll recognize danger signals before the red light flashes, such as the absolute folly of going into a business for which you are not prepared. And I hope you'll see once again that preparation, vision and good management pay off in dollars. These principles are far more important than many people are willing to admit.

Four big factors to consider

What are the elements of the ideal enterprise? More or less, they are: (1) a public need; (2) low overhead; (3) rapid turnover; (4) permanent demand. Seldom will you find an enterprise that is really ideal. The closer it approaches, the better.

In selecting the field he wants to enter, it is important for the young man to try to select a field which has a future. For example, there would not be a vast opportunity in being a feather merchant today, or in manufacturing horse collars or buggies.

Again, the average individual, in determining upon a business career, thinks of the conventional fields in which there is usually severe competition. Other persons have made substantial incomes and occasionally even small fortunes by looking to the unusual occupation. It is more sound economically to look to the needs of the community or nation and then to engage in the field which serves that need.

A few years ago, I was brought into contact with an organization in Kankakee, Illinois, known as the L & S Bait Company, a manufacturer of artificial lures. This was started as a basement enterprise in 1942. It has now grown to sizable proportions, and it became an enterprise of great value to its founders. One would think of this as a trivial field, one which could never amount to great consequence, yet the mere field of artificial bait for fishermen has brought them success far beyond any possible expectation which they may have had.

A hobby can become a business

Of course, one should seek in his work not only financial success but the doing of that which he enjoys. I know a lawyer in Iowa who is an ardent gardener, who has devoted most of his spare time to trying to develop early blooming chrysanthemums. He has succeeded and is now selling plants commercially. Another individual is a gun hobbyist, and started a gun shop which he runs only in the evenings and on weekends. In fact, he doesn't like to work too well, so he doesn't do much the rest of the time, but he makes an excellent income from his shop and has as customers people of similar taste with whom he holds bull sessions at a profit which he formerly held at home, without profit.

Other persons have been successful in personal service enterprises by establishing shopping and gift purchasing establishments, which aid the busy male (and also keep a file of his anniversary and important dates, to avoid the penalties of forgetfulness), party and entertainment services, orchestra booking offices, nursing agencies, baby sitting agencies, employment agencies, nurseries, tutoring facilities, athletic instruction, health studios, dancing schools, and charm schools. These are merely a few fields where often a considerable need exists.

★   *But the great need of each of us is not ordinarily to succeed in the unconventional but to solve more deftly the problems which arise in our more conventional tasks—whether it be as a manufacturer, a banker, or a merchandiser.*

The seller of goods or services of any type must be a man of many facets—an advertiser, skilled buyer, economist, prophet, executive, and salesman. Let us glance briefly at some of those enterprises in which one may be called upon to work, or to initiate his own business, or to invest.

Opportunities in wholesaling

Some of the most stable and profitable business enterprises are in the category of wholesaling, jobbing, and commission houses. In retail establishments, the proprietor usually must gamble upon a certain specialized market picture for some little period of time. Normally, although there is some variation in particular enterprises, the wholesaler or middleman stands between the production source and the retail outlet, purchasing only enough of a given commodity to meet the needs of his customers, without the necessity of stocking enough of any particular supply on hand so as to run any major risk. A magazine distributor, for example, returns the unsold copies. He does not stand the loss. A large drug distribution house does not have the investment of personally manufacturing the items which it sells, but primarily only the expense of its own operation, which is that of distribution.

The major requirement which confronts the wholesale outlet, other than developing its sources of supply and its customers, is that of capital necessary to pay for the items purchased (if they are not purchased on consignment), or at least to carry the cost thereof after delivery has been made and until payment is received from the customer. With an established enterprise, most of these funds come from bank loans predicated upon inventories of accounts receivable, or both.

There is a definite risk of loss, however, where a wholesaler or distributor deals in perishables. In such an instance, there is a possibility of a loss through deterioration of the product, either because of its inherent nature, or because of loss caused by strikes, lockouts, lack of shipping facilities, war, and other factors. There is also a danger in perishables which may fluctuate widely upon the market, such as in cotton. Insurance may be carried, of course, to guard against possible hazards of fire, windstorm, flood, theft, or other casualties.

Retailing: Business at a different level

The difference between wholesale operations and retail operations can, in general, be illustrated by glancing at the difference between the retail lumberyard and the lumber broker. A retail lumberyard must, first, own a piece of property to which customers can come. Upon this property it must have trackage facilities for a railroad to bring in its lumber. It must have an office building of some type and at least one storage shed where lumber is protected against the elements. All of this costs money; and, in addition, it must stock large quantities of lumber of different types in varying dimensions and grades. It must also stock millwork, hardware, paints, and other articles which it sells. If the lumberyard has purchased while the market was low, it may stand to profit by a sharp increase in price. But it must reorder constantly, and if it has to buy when prices are high, a sharp drop in prices will definitely hurt. A lumber broker, on the other hand, keeps abreast of prices daily. He either has current orders from his customers when he calls the Pacific coast for its fir, redwood, Ponderosa pine, cedar, and plywood, or the South for its yellow pine or white pine, or the broker knows where the carloads which he purchases can be sold. These cars can then be diverted en route to the desired destination. Or he can order cars made up to the specifications of a certain customer. A lumber broker operating in this manner requires comparatively small capital.

Integrity—or else

The same is largely true of grain brokers who purchase, over the telephone, grain from local elevators and resell the next moment by telephone to the Board of Trade. Any dealer of this sort must be the type of individual to whom his own integrity and reputation are most precious. Some years ago, I owned an interest in a grain elevator which bought and sold corn, purchasing from farmers and reselling through brokers. The transactions were all verbal. A farmer welched upon a deal to sell 5,000 bushels of corn, but it did not even occur to us to use that as an excuse not to fulfill our agreement to sell. That verbal agreement was fulfilled at a loss of several thousand dollars. One must have the same feeling as Henry Peterson, of Feature Ring, when he said:

> "I've never been ashamed to face up to any business dealing I have been in, or to own up to any work I've ever produced." *

Turning to retail establishments, the same general principles would, of course, apply to them. The proprietor must be a person of integrity whose reputation builds and maintains his clientele. He should be a good salesman, with an appealing personality, able to attract and hold a following. He must be alert, imaginative, and cognizant of the value of catchy advertising. But, most important, *he must know the business intimately*. If he does not, the mistakes he makes in purchasing merchandise, in pricing merchandise, and in the general operation of the business will eat up his capital before he has become proficient in that line.

★   *A man would be foolish to enter into the business of selling plumbing supplies, if he knows nothing about that enterprise. Or, can one conceive of a person entering the field of selling ladies' dresses who does not know where to buy the merchandise, what type of merchandise to buy, the number of dresses to acquire in each size, and the other hundred-and-one problems which exist in that field?*

* *Operation Success*, p. 166.

Keeping track of money

One must know how to create credit. He must also know how to pay off his bills. For example, sometimes the margin of net profit comes in the discounts secured by the prompt payment of bills. Absent this profit factor, and he may go broke. He must keep his taxes paid. Many proprietors have gotten into difficulties solely by reason of the fact of using government money for their operations, such as sales taxes which they collect from customers, or withholding taxes or unemployment compensation taxes which should be paid upon employees. Rather than borrow to meet a payroll, or to pay for a particular purchase, they use that money, which is the same as dipping one's hand in another man's till.

Other persons, in operating businesses, have permitted their accounts receivable to amount to totals which keep them stripped of operating capital, and in time a large proportion of old accounts become uncollectible. Several years ago, a local plumber presented his problem to me and asked me if he was entitled to charge interest on overdue accounts. I suggested an alternative to him, which has worked splendidly. I told him that, instead of charging interest, people always like to receive discounts. Therefore, instead of marking up an overdue account, simply mark up his bill 10% to start with, and then stamp boldly on each bill that a discount of 10%, setting it out in dollars, would be given if the bill is paid within 15 days. Almost all persons pay promptly to secure the discount.

The need is the thing

One shortcut to success in retail business activities is to select a line where a definite shortage exists. One can analyze the needs of the community, in determining where such a shortage lies. However, any good business, soundly operated, can succeed against the most vigorous competition. For example, in an average community, dozens of stores will sell toys. Suppose, however, that a person should open a store colorfully designed and call it "Santa's Workshop." If it is designed and decorated in such a manner as to make it immediately appealing to children, half the battle would be won. The children, themselves, would make the business a success and their powers of persuading parents should not be underrated. In addition, if it handled every conceivable type of toy for the child of ten years of age or less, the parent normally would head directly for that store instead of going from one place of business to another.

The amount of profit made by retail stores may be wholly disproportionate to the amount of invested capital, or even to the resale value. Julia Meadows, for example, has a dress shop. She doesn't own the building; her investment in equipment and in merchandise amounts to about $15,000. Yet she takes out quite a bit more than that in net profit each year. Still there are other stores which have investments in excess of $40,000 which produce less than $10,000 a year net to their proprietors. The difference lies partly in the type of business—even more, however, in the personality of the proprietor and the type of clientele established. One should not invest in a retail business of any type, however, unless he has full knowledge of the operations performed and of the individuals operating the business. Misplaced confidence can mean a flat pocketbook. One had better, if asked to invest, act only upon expert advice. As Leopold Silberstein stated:

"I have used experts all my life. I cannot say that everything I have done on their advice has been 100 per cent right, but this I can say—nothing I have ever done has been a 100 per cent lemon!" *

Again, one may develop a type of business designed exclusively to meet the needs of certain trades, businesses, or

* *Operation Success*, p. 19.

professions. Woody Colwell, in Champaign, Illinois, has a publishing house and service which prints forms, reports, statements, books and records for physicians, together with an advisory service dealing with accounting and other problems peculiar to their work. Similar services exist with reference to almost every class of business—yet, there are still openings in this respect. These needs can be determined from one's personal knowledge or from talking to friends in diversified employments. What are their needs? What types of services could be offered? What would be a fair price for such service—or, in other words, what will offer a fair profit to the entrepreneur without overtaxing the customer? A tax service to an attorney may cost $75 a year or more, but a service to a small clothing retailer may not be salable at more than a third of this amount. Such fields must be carefully analyzed before entering into them; and then, of course, one must be qualified to render the service which is needed. This, itself, calls for expert knowledge.

One man's meat

For some reason, whenever a retiring athlete considers establishing a business to operate when his athletic career has ended, he seems to hit upon the restaurant business. Some succeed, many fail. The drawing power of his name fades quickly, and the restaurant business demands expert knowledge and skilled supervision.

One who establishes a successful restaurant business, if his ambition so spurs him, can conceivably develop it into a successful chain operation. Usually, this is accomplished by selecting certain favorite types of foods, using standard recipes, combining purchasing power for reduced cost, and using a standardized style of architecture and a trade name so that satisfied customers in one area will stop at other branches while travelling. Also, the advertising value of each helps to expand the business potential of the others. But, whether one enters the restaurant business upon a nationwide basis or in a single location, he must recognize that this business is highly competitive, although the competition is often of low caliber. Usually one need not consider as serious competition the many shacks and dives, frequently having some unappealing sign such as "Good Eats." Other restaurateurs find it impossible to combine good food and atmosphere into a single package. Those proprietors should examine the problems presented from the point of view of the one looking for an attractive place to dine, and solutions would usually appear. Each of these matters is fundamental; no one can afford to ignore them.

I have been told by a restaurant operator that a liquor license generally produces more revenue than the food served in the restaurant. That, I believe, is understandable, because the comparative expense of materials, as well as of service involved in liquor versus food, is much smaller. The proprietor should be just as discriminating in securing excellent liquor recipes as he is in the selection of his food recipes, and only good grades of beverages should be used in mixed drinks. The individual flagon holding martinis, manhattans, etc., has come to have great customer appeal.

I am firmly convinced that it is the woman who normally decides where a couple will go to dine. From the feminine point of view, I find that Jean, for example, is interested primarily in restaurants which serve delicious hot breads, excellent salads, and delectable and different desserts. Most restaurants, and many hotel dining rooms, skimp upon these items.

Class always tells

Repeatedly I have seen new restaurants established upon sound principles practically strip long existing competitors of the cream of their business within the short space of a few months. Word of mouth advertising is most potent. Of course, it helps from the point of view of transient trade to have a good recommendation in the AAA list and those of other services. And, unfortunately, I have also seen restaurants which have risen to popularity most quickly slide to an all-time low as the proprietor felt he could then start to cheapen his foods or his service; and, in that event, the disappointed customer seldom returns.

It has long seemed to me that places which cater to luncheon business make a mistake in sticking either to sandwiches and soups, or else full course luncheons. There are scores of excellent light luncheons which can be served at reasonable prices, which would be much more welcome to the average white-collar worker, whether male or female. There are restaurants rapidly coming into popularity which employ a buffet style, where a person can select as much or as little as he desires. Some of these are developing as chains—as for example, the "dine-a-terias."

The personality of the proprietor is, of course, important. It is clear that a man who is taciturn by nature, or inhibited in his dealings with others (in other words, a sourpuss), should not go into the restaurant business. He must be an outgoing, pleasant type of person. If he is going to be in contact work, people must like him.

Convenience counts

Departing from conventional restaurants, I would like to point out that during depression days college boys who could not earn more than four dollars a day in arduous labor frequently would open a roadside hamburger and ice cream stand and make enough during the summer vacation to pay the following year's expenses. This fact, as such, is not important—but the principle which it illustrates is of great importance. That is, that people travelling do not want to take time to go into a business section for better food—but will stop at a roadside place to conserve both time and money. Drive-in restaurants located at major highway intersections are developing rapidly and doing well. Entire chains of the Steak-N-Shake, Pig-N-Whistle, Dairy Queen, and Dog n

Suds are developing rapidly; "Chicken in a Basket" is a familiar sign. Even local residents frequently will go to a drive-in and, perhaps, eat in the car to avoid hunting for parking places or to avoid having to get dressed or shaved. This suggests that more elaborate restaurants would do well to have adequate parking facilities.

I mentioned above the Dog n Suds business. Here, in his own words, is what Don Hamacher said about it:

"Several years ago Jim and I started the first Dog n Suds Drive-In as a means of augmenting our meager teaching salaries.

"The first summer open, we were able to make $8,000 between us, and, because of our success, many people asked if they couldn't open a Dog n Suds Drive-In.

"We asked ourselves if it wouldn't be possible to help others get into this profitable business. Right there the 'Dog n Suds Idea' was born."

They now sell franchises to establish new branches to their chain, furnishing equipment, supplies, signs, and even the building. The same is true with iced custard and other chain food dispensaries, such as Tastee-Freez. They tell the retailer what to do and make him do it, because it naturally would disturb them if he did not make money. I am told that some such retail outlets make over $10,000 in an eight-month year.

Contracting? Go slow

Almost every carpenter who becomes disgruntled with his boss believes that the pot of gold at the end of the rainbow is waiting for him if he only becomes a contractor. This is not necessarily so bad, if he is familiar with material prices and the work of various subcontractors. But the belief that a fortune is waiting just around the corner for anyone who enters the contracting business is a delusion which ensnares many persons each year.

Five years ago, I knew Jimmy Brown, a real estate man

who was a born salesman, who possessed a world of charm and who, before he was thirty, had three other real estate salesmen working for him. However, at that time I met Jimmy because I had to set up a program to keep him out of bankruptcy, so that he could pay off his creditors upon the installment plan. Jimmy had succumbed to the delusion that he was a contractor, and had lost his shirt. He promised me solemnly that he would never enter the contracting field again. He returned to his full time activity of selling real estate, and again prospered, but two years ago Jimmy busted higher than a kite—he had again turned contractor.

A lawyer friend of mine in another community has just managed to drop $18,000 in cash, and about $30,000 of useful time had he spent it in the law business, in setting up a contracting business and watching the dollars run out through a hole in the bottom. For each twenty new persons whom I see enter the contracting business, about four or five do pretty well, eight manage to make a subsistence, and the others go broke. It is not, ordinarily, a business for amateurs; it is a skilled calling, requiring expert knowledge, hard work, and considerable native shrewdness.

Now that all prospective persons have been warned off from that field, let me tell you the story of a person who made a success of contracting. It is a team story, of a man and his wife. Their names are Cecil and Gleena Ozier.

In the early 1930's, Cecil was a clerk for the Illinois Central Railroad Company. He didn't make much money at it, but there was job security. However, they could not manage to save enough to buy a new home. They studied all sorts of plans and designs for the type of small home they would like to build; they shopped around to learn about materials and how to use them; and finally, with Cecil acting as his own contractor, and hiring a minimum of subcontracting help, they built their home. They built it, surprisingly enough, for considerably less than they had dared hope, with both of them doing much of the work themselves.

"I want one too"

A couple visiting in their home a few months later fell in love with it and wanted to know if Cecil could build such a home for them. The upshot of it was that Cecil and Gleena sold their home and built another. They moved into that, and in a few months had to move again, but with each move they were building up capital.

In a short time, Cecil was building a few homes upon speculation. He had studied everything he could learn about the building trade, while Gleena had studied interior decorating, color harmony, and the little touches necessary to add charm to a home. Cecil did not give up his job with the railroad; for a great many years he kept his seniority, but he did take a leave of absence. As each house was finished, he persuaded merchants to furnish it completely, and it was advertised as a "model home." Hundreds of people traipsed through these houses upon weekends, resulting in sales of furniture and effects placed in the homes by the merchants, and the sales of the homes which Cecil had built.

In each of these instances, he was careful not to build enormous homes, but attractive homes of three or four bedrooms in desirable residential areas, convenient to transportation, schools, and parks. Never did he skimp by placing such homes in undesirable locations. If the same plan was used in more than one location, it was always varied in appearance—such as by reversing the arrangement, putting one exterior in stone with another in brick, or by so situating it that it looked different.

Cecil's contracting business expanded rapidly until World War II closed down private building. At that time, he entered the field of public housing of the type required for the housing of soldiers, civilian employees, and others. It was a new field for him, but he knew costs and he knew construction. As a result, he prospered. After the war, he was ready for the boom in small, low down payment housing, and he entered upon it on a large scale, building hundreds of such homes, but not forgetting to vary the exteriors and the appearance and arrangement of those houses in order to bestow individuality upon each. Sure, those last houses are not as lovely and charming as the houses he first built; but they are in a vastly different price range, and they did provide housing which was badly needed.

Luck had nothing to do with it

Since that time, his enterprises have grown and expanded —he is, in fact, building slab cast concrete houses in Puerto Rico, and is planning others in South America. He is building a village for retired people in Florida, and his local and more distant enterprises continue to boom. But it was not a situation of an inexperienced railroad clerk getting lucky; it was a team proposition of a man and wife working very hard, and sacrificing, for what they wanted to do, and then working diligently and intelligently toward the fulfillment of their goal.

Trend is to mass housing

The day of the conventional contractor seems to be moving on. The trend is more and more to pre-cut and prefabricated homes. That is not necessarily bad. As I pointed out before, house construction is one thing in which up until fifteen years ago, there were few advances over the last 2,000 years. Houses usually become obsolescent before they fall down, and perhaps it should be recognized that homes should be replaced every few decades, just as automobiles are usually replaced every few years.

At any rate, there is no question but that modern techniques of production have greatly lowered the acquisition cost of pre-fab homes, and the conventional contractor cannot compete with the dealer who handles the factory product at a comparatively small markup with a minimum of local labor. Since the aim is to get as many people as possible into their own homes, at comparatively low cost, business realities determine that one is normally better off to secure a dealership for a good line, compute his costs accurately, arrange sound sales methods, and set up reserves for any future repairs or guarantees which might be required. However, this cannot condone the tens of thousands of jerry-built homes which have been sold to young couples, in particular; and pending prosecutions indicate that some steps are being taken to end housing frauds of this type.

Big digging

There is quite a different phase of contracting which is to be distinguished from house construction, or private contracting. This is the business of public contracting. Public contracting deals with many facets of a business demanding, by and large, the use of heavy equipment. Highway construction is one of the major phases of such activity; bridge building, drainage work, sewer and drain tile construction are other facets of this business; and the erection of large public buildings is a final phase.

This is a highly competitive industry, one in which fortunes have been made, and lost, with rapidity. The usual requisite for the securing of contracts is that one be the low bidder, assuming that his financial resources and reputation qualify him for the job, and that a reputable bonding company will bond him. If one bids too high, he secures no contract; if he bids too low, he faces bankruptcy. Often a single job involves large enough sums that a gross underestimate could close his doors.

It is advisable for a public contractor to be a graduate architectural engineer or civil engineer. Some extremely successful public contractors, however, have been men with extensive experience in working for others in that field, until they have come to know it intimately themselves. Usually no one but the owner of the business has sufficient background to prepare the estimates; and, since a mistake can break him, usually he will guard against errors. Some men have made fortunes in public contracting, of course, because of close political ties with the powers who control the letting of bids, but that is often in violation of law. Since public contracting firms depend so greatly upon the abilities of one man, or of two men, the loss of retirement of such men can mean catastrophe.

With all the importance of knowing your field, it still is quite possible to go into a new field and make a success. But —and this is a big "but"—you must study the new field so thoroughly that it becomes as familiar as the old.

PRACTICAL POINTERS

1. If you can, pick a field where there is little competition—or where you can offer enough to override competition. In all events, pick a field with a future.
2. There is wholesale and there is retail, and they are different in many ways. A business that is not good for you at the retail level may be very good at the wholesale level, or vice versa.
3. You can learn both by other people's success and by their failures and mistakes. The restaurant business is a good case in point.
4. Whatever you do, know what you're doing. Know backward and forward, inside and out, what you are doing.

7

You Can Succeed Through
Better Service

ONE WAY TO MAKE MONEY is to educate or train yourself to perform a service needed by others. Instead of working with a capital asset or commodity, one works with knowledge or highly developed skills. In these fields we find our professional men, our salesmen, our brokers.

There is one disadvantage, as well as one advantage, to such enterprises. In the professions, in particular, one may spend years of time and many thousands of dollars in training for his life's work. If he is cut off in his prime by accident or disease, his widow has no assets to sell. His abilities, his knowledge, his personality, and his memory were his assets and those perished with him. The widow of a manufacturer or retailer is more fortunate in this respect in that there is a physical asset of value. Similarly, upon retirement, the professional man's income usually ceases when his efforts cease. That is not necessarily true of one who owns a business entity. It may continue its work, even when his personal labors end.

On the other hand, the creation of the business enterprise represents an investment over the years. Not only is initial capital usually required, but almost all liquid funds are poured into the business during one's active career. Even though the businessman or manufacturer receives substantial amounts of money, and is required to pay tax upon that income, he may nevertheless lack the enjoyment of spending the money which he feels his business requires. A farmer with a huge and well-painted barn and small unpainted house portrays this situation. A professional man, apart from the initial investment in his training, may have more spendable income as he proceeds through life.

In considering whether or not one should train for a profession, the first thing a man or woman must consider is his native ability. It takes an excellent mind, in the first instance, and at least not a distaste for schooling, in order to pursue the many years of training which is required. One who has deft, sure hands, steady nerves, and great patience may be well equipped for surgery. A person whose fingers are all thumbs, as are mine, but who likes people, has a knack for putting words together, has a fairly logical mind, and who has a large slice of ham in his makeup will often make a good trial lawyer, or possibly an actor, lecturer, or salesman. Other attributes may turn one toward engineering, or architecture, or journalism, or the arts. Personal abilities, whatever they may be, should be utilized to the best advantage. If one is in doubt, vocational guidance may be of definite advantage.

Today, science is king

There is no question but that the trend of today's civilization is toward the sciences. Men who are well trained in engineering, chemistry, chemical engineering, physics, and other phases of the sciences have a tremendous demand for their services. They are assured of lucrative positions, almost complete financial security, and an excellent future. Nevertheless, there are many people whose temperaments do not qualify them for the sciences, and in the rush toward the specialized, one is often prone to lose sight of the fact that others have opportunities for excellent careers in those businesses and professions which will continue on, irrespective of emphasis or de-emphasis of technology.

Let us take the medical profession for example. There is, at present, a tremendous shortage of physicians, and there will continue to be this shortage so long as we continue to have inadequate facilities for the training of young physicians. Yet we cannot get more trainees without more extensive physical facilities, more medical teachers, and expanded curricula without cheapening the standards presently followed. This means, necessarily, that the income of the physician is high. According to most recent figures, the average income of physicians is almost double that of attorneys. It has more than quadrupled in the period from 1940 to 1963.

A physician can live well

The training period of medical men and attorneys is roughly the same. Assuming that one can make the grade in medical school, then, from the point of view of monetary return alone, his financial opportunities would seem to be greater in medicine than in law. Analyzing the field of medicine more in detail, we find that surgeons are more highly compensated than diagnosticians, and that specialists earn more than general practitioners. Surgeons operating in a specialized or difficult field where there is a great need for their services have the greatest command of high fees. Therefore, again speaking of money return alone, the individual who selects a specialized field of surgery in which he establishes a good reputation usually commands a high income. A physician may also establish a clinic and expand services offered through the group, thus realizing income not only from his own efforts but from the efforts of the men associated with him, although those men may thereby also share in his income.

We are fortunate in having extremely high standards of medical care in this community. Back in the mid '30's, a group of Mayo-trained men established a clinic and hospital in Urbana which soon became known as "little Mayo's." As the number of men with it increased, and the reputations of the physicians expanded, it began to draw from a radius of downstate Illinois and Indiana. Most of the men identified with it were Board men. A competing clinic in Champaign created similarly high standards to maintain competition with the Urbana clinic, and the independent physicians were required thereby to elevate and to maintain their standards, as well. As a result of such competition we have more physicians per 1,000 persons in this community than the nationwide average, of extremely high stature in their specialties, and yet the incomes of these men are proportionately high. Accordingly, the mere fact of competition does not necessarily reduce income, but may be beneficial to all.

Professions have a business side

The physician must consider how he is going to conduct his professional practice, whether it will be as (a) an employee, either of a corporation, a clinic, or a partnership; (b) a sole practitioner; or (c) a member of a clinic, association, or other entity. Such a decision depends largely upon the individual himself—his type of practice, his personalty, his energy, his gregariousness, and other factors. Each physician must make a determination for himself, taking into consideration his objectives in life, his personality, and the opportunities afforded.

If that physician decides to join forces with another or with several doctors, it is imperative that any lasting relationship must be built upon solid rock. It must be established between individuals who both respect and like each other thoroughly, who are equally energetic and willing to assume responsibility, and whose integrity is above reproach.

If a partnership is determined upon, the relationships should be spelled out in a detailed written agreement drawn to clarify any reasonably probable contingencies. These should include, for example, as to what happens if either physician is called or recalled into military service, what happens in the event of the temporary disability of either or in the event of the long-lasting disability of either, what is to occur in the event either should die, retire, or decide to dissolve the partnership.

If a clinic is established, it should likewise clarify the relationships of the employing members and of the employee members. There must be an opportunity for the younger physicians to advance within the organization, to increase their earnings, and to visualize a secure and enjoyable future. An approved pension plan is often a splendid asset to possess, and in such event Uncle Sam helps pay the bill.

Who owns the customers?

In this connection, and this must be borne in mind in practically every business or profession, it must be realized that any employee or associate dealing with patients, clients, or customers of any enterprise soon comes to regard those persons as his individual following. When an employee has developed a sufficient following, often he quits and opens up a competitive establishment.

There is only one way in which the employer can protect himself from such competition. That is by having a written contract containing a non-competition agreement reasonable in scope as to location and duration. Actually, in most instances, a period of one year and a limitation to the county where the business is located will suffice. The employee will not desire to remain unemployed for a year and usually will go elsewhere, if he resigns. Even if he returns after one year, the so-called following will have become used to his absence and will have continued to deal with the employer. While the former employee may pick up a remnant of such following, it will not be dangerously large. But it is important that such agreement be written and not verbal.

Other medical fields

It frequently happens that one cannot secure admittance to a medical school for one of many reasons—either because his grades are not high enough, because of the tremendous number of applications for the few vacancies which exist, because his financial resources are not adequate, or for other reasons. In such event, if his bent is still toward dealing with physical ailments, he may find a lucrative field in osteopathy, chiropractic, chiropody, optometry, dentistry, physio-therapy, or related fields. In many states the standing of osteopaths has advanced to the point where they help fill part of the need which exists because of the shortage of medical doctors. In each and all of these fields, success depends largely upon one's ability, energy, and personality. I can name men right in our community in each of the major fields so designated who have made what others would regard as comfortable fortunes.

There is a sharp rise, also, in the demand for the services of veterinarians and in their relative incomes. In farm states, such as Illinois, there is always a major demand for veterinarian services in dealing with livestock, but there is an even greater demand for their services from the owners of pets. When one figures out the total pet population within any given community, the cost of distemper shots, the cost of annual rabies shots, the cost of those little operations designed to keep down the population of dogdom or catdom, and the many other services required, plus the need of boarding facilities, it is seen that there is a large gross revenue available. In my own opinion, a veterinarian renders a great deal of service and skill for a proportionately small charge.

The law as a career

Going now to the practice of law, in past years the returns from the practice of law were often overrated by laymen. Generally it takes many years, following the completion of years of study, before a young lawyer develops a clientele. Most lawyers never attain wealth. Of those who do, wealth is usually obtained not through practice but through business opportunities with which they come into contact in their practices. For example, Adlai Rust, president of the State Farm Mutual Automobile Insurance Company, was an excellent attorney practicing in Bloomington, Illinois. George J. Mecherle, founder of the insurance company, consulted him as a client, and Adlai rode along upon a nominal basis with the company during its formative years. Eventually, it demanded so much of his time that he became executive vice-president and treasurer, and has now succeeded to the presidency. A like history could be given for many other successful executives, who have stepped from the law into business of one phase or another, or who own substantial interests in a number of enterprises founded by their clients, with their assistance, legal or financial, or both.

More and more need for lawyers

The competition in the field of law is not so bad as it was twenty years ago. The need for legal services has been constantly increasing with the complexity in our tax laws, administrative tribunals, and each governmental step taken to simplify our lives. Yet, while the demand for legal service has been increasing, the supply of attorneys has been going down. In 1950 there were 13,641 new attorneys admitted to practice. In 1953, the number had dropped to 10,976, and in 1956 to 9,450. In 1962, the number again declined despite a tremendous population surge.

When I concluded my law studies in 1934, in the city

of Chicago they were employing young attorneys at a salary
of $75 a month in some top offices and $50 a month in others,
while most young attorneys could not get jobs in practice at
all. Some offices were permitting young lawyers to work
there simply for experience. I was considered to have picked
off a plum when I started at $125 a month. Almost every law
graduate now can secure a good opportunity at a starting
salary which belies the "starvation period"; and, even if he
goes into practice for himself, can usually get sufficient referred business from older lawyers to keep busy.

Striking out alone

If the lawyer intends to go into practice by himself, there
are three things which he should normally consider. First, if
he has close connections with a business which can feed to
him a large volume of legal work, his chances are good in
that community. The usual type of situation involves a father
who is president of a bank or who has a manufacturing company which requires a good deal of legal work. Second, if
the young attorney has no connections at all, the quickest
way to establish a clientele is to go to a small community
which either has no lawyers or a few older men not desiring
to work too hard. A following may then be quickly built
up; and, as a rule, the older lawyer will send many cases
to the beginner, which they deem will require hard work or
bring small fees. Third, if a lawyer aspires to success in a
larger community but has no connections, he must develop a
reputation as a specialist which will bring other lawyers, as
well as private clients, into his office.

Tax lawyer's progress

An illustration of the last situation would be in connection
with taxation law. This is rapidly becoming one of the most
important and lucrative fields of practice. A young lawyer
can take a position with the Internal Revenue Department

working as a field man, then as a reviewing officer, next as an attorney in Washington working with contested cases, and finally as a trial man. During this time, let us say four or five years, he may study intensively and read everything written in the field. Perhaps he writes a few articles, or even a book, upon some phase of taxation law. When our young tax lawyer is ready to enter private practice, he is an expert who not only understands the basic law but who understands the procedures followed by the government and its attitude upon various types of taxation problems. Charles Davis, former general counsel of the Internal Revenue Service, when he resumed private practice in the city of Chicago, was still less than 40 years of age despite the distinguished post he had occupied.

One of the present shortages in the legal field has been in trial law. I used to believe that trial lawyers were made; I am now inclined to believe that they are born. For the top-flight trial lawyer, it takes a certain temperament and natural ability, in addition to intensive preparation and constant study. For the person who loves such work, it is exciting and rewarding.

Another field of specialty is that of patent law. Again, with the emphasis upon technology, this has become a rapidly increasing field. At one time, almost anyone could be admitted to the practice of patent law, whether an attorney or not. The standards for admission to practice are constantly being elevated. One young lawyer friend of mine, LeRoy Richards, entering the practice of patent law as a novice, received more as a starting salary than the dean of the College of Law of the University of Illinois received when I was a student there. Of course, these are merely illustrations as to the various fields of specialization in the practice of law. There are many others. Unusual knowledge, or unusual abilities, in any field should always pay dividends.

★   *One thing which a student in any professional field, or in any business herein discussed, should consider in first getting started is "Where do I want to live the rest of my life?" If he possesses ability, he can do well in any given geographical location. But it is an expensive business to tear up roots after building up a following of any kind and to reestablish a business or practice in a community where one is unknown. This involves starting all over again. In addition, such states as California, Florida, and Arizona do not admit a lawyer or a doctor to practice merely because he has practiced elsewhere. Often he must move to that state and live there a minimum period of time, usually a year. Then he must take a special examination in which the percentage of failure is high. All other things being equal, it is generally a good idea to attend a university in the state where one intends to live. And in making the decision as to the place of permanent residence one should consider such matters as climate, scenic beauty, recreational facilities, and other circumstances which help to make life enjoyable.*

Getting back to personal service occupations, other folks find their particular niches in such things as architecture, art, music, writing, and other fields. Again, in this community, it has become somewhat of a center for distinguished architects. With the proper training, good ideas, willingness to work, and sales ability, architects have been quite successful at youthful ages. With all of the public and private building now going on, there is a tremendous need for architects and men of vision, and one can find both satisfaction and financial reward in this field.

Why artists live in attics

Apart from the field of architecture, it is somewhat unfortunate for the arts that the old patron system has disappeared. Leaving out of our consideration popular or dance music, only about one per cent of artists, musicians, and writers are able to make even a moderate living from those fields. In almost every instance, their livelihoods must be made through teaching, one of the professions, or work of other types, in order to indulge the luxury of the arts. It is only when such a person has received particular recognition, either through unusual talent, fortunate breaks, or carefully planned publicity that such activity ordinarily will bring in substantial rewards. None of these fields is ideal for the purpose of this book which involves primarily the attainment of financial security.

An accountant has an important job

The field of accounting is another field which may present unusual opportunities, because of the intimacy of contact with a number of other fields. In this regard, I am reminded of a dialogue which occurred between Walter Chrysler and a young man who came to him for advice as to an occupation to enter.

"You come to me for advice?"
"Yes, sir."
"All right, son, you are going to get some: You know this country is filled with developing industries. And there are lots of chances. You simply want to make yourself smart enough to recognize them before the other fellow does. If I were you, I'd qualify myself for accountancy. I'd become an accountant. Young accountants are sent around by their firms to audit the books of companies everywhere. They have a skill that makes them mighty valuable in business; indispensable. They often get chances

to go to work for the companies whose books they have audited." *

And there is a great deal of sound sense in that advice. An accountant, in any event, can make an excellent per diem income. His work may lead him into many other opportunities, and normally he has an intimacy of knowledge of that business through his books and records which prevents him from being fooled about its condition or future. But one must enjoy such meticulous and detailed work if he is to be successful in it. I am sure that I would never have passed Accounting in college, if one of my friends had not been teaching the course.

★   *The one single field of personal endeavor which I consider offers the greatest field for financial return, with a minimum of expense in preparing for it, is sales work. The income of salesmen is always at the top of the particular business in which they are engaged. One reason is that most people dread sales work. They underestimate their own abilities to sell; and, visualizing a successful salesman as a high pressure individual, feel that they cannot qualify.*

Selling may be better than you think

The high pressure man does not last long with any organization. He is distrusted by customers; he secures no substantial repeat business. The ordinary fellow, who makes a respectable appearance, who is friendly and honest in his statements, and who knows his product, is the one who consistently brings home the bacon. And, of course, the steady increase in one's following builds up repeat business which goes on from year to year without undue effort.

* *Life of an American Workman*, p. 178.

Necessarily, the amount of revenue received by a salesman will depend upon the product which he sells, its quality, the demand therefor, the amount of time used in going from customer to customer, the price of the product, and the commission rate. A person selling a high-priced product for which there is great demand, at a substantial commission rate, can attain wealth easily. On the other hand, a salesman peddling can openers from door to door may starve. The prospective salesman must study the potentialities of a product before giving it his allegiance.

By way of further emphasis, it is apparent that a person who sells a $50,000 machine will make a larger commission than one selling a $10 book. However, the time and money expended to make the first sale may be extremely great. After months of build-up, the deal may collapse. And big deals may be made by the executives of the two organizations involved, leaving no direct opportunity for the salesman.

But normally I have found that a man who can sell one thing can sell another. I have sold books, silk stockings, and photographs—and my primary work now is selling my clients' views to juries. The same qualities of sincerity, clarity of presentation, and inducing conviction apply to all aspects of sales work.

A big-money job

In almost every industry, sales managers and crack salesmen rank at the income peak. They are coddled, as well, because they are the producers of the gross income upon which the business depends. Nor does selling usually require special educational training, except in the technological industries. Even one who has never graduated from high school can become an excellent salesman, if he dresses moderately well, overcomes improprieties in speech, and develops his cultural background. One man of my acquaintance has made extraordinary strides in the last year through work in a Dale Carnegie course.

Of course, it is not necessary for a salesman to work for an employer. The same qualities which make for success in that employment are highly essential ingredients in almost any business, frequently spelling the difference between success and failure.

Selling for yourself

If the individual wants to concentrate exclusively upon sales work and remain self-employed, with a minimum of capital, the fields suggested immediately are real estate and insurance. These may be combined, ordinarily, although in certain instances they must be limited to one business alone.

To start in the real estate business, all that one needs is a license and a telephone. Next, he needs listings. One of the first steps is to contact and make friends of as many attorneys as possible. They run into potential listings frequently which they pass along to agents in whom they have confidence. Again, it is well to send an interesting announcement to selected persons listed in the local telephone directory. Whether they have business at that time or not, often they will remember the agent's name. Next, it is well to take an ample advertisement in the classified section of the telephone directory where it will catch the eye of strangers or of persons having no allegiance to a competitive firm. If one's name starts with "Z," since many persons start calling the first agent listed, it is not a bad idea to give such agency a trade name such as "Allied Realtors" or "Acme Realty Company, John Zuchok, manager." If legal regulations require the listing of such trade name with a state or local office, do so immediately.

The average rate on real estate sales is 5%, with a lower rate on farm properties. Therefore, it is advisable for one to concentrate on homes in the lower brackets, which move more quickly than large homes, thus amassing a larger total.

In addition to property sales, of course, rentals may be an important income producer. Normally this is too time-consuming to be of special interest except as a part of a management service for apartment buildings. Upon these, the prevailing rate in Illinois is 10% of gross income, and the manager usually earns his fee. However, a young man just entering business may find that such earnings will feed his family while he is becoming established.

Connections count

In addition, it is well to have connections with the loan departments of insurance companies. Most property buyers require financing, which gives the real estate agent an inside track for procuring such loan with almost no additional effort. The usual commission is ½ of 1% of the loan, although in some cases it may run higher. Becoming an accredited loan agent and appraiser will help to produce higher returns. And the annual service fees upon loans may quickly build up into a profitable annual income.

It was only a few years ago that Jean and I were having dinner with a young attorney and his wife. He is an awfully nice guy who does not like the hubbub or competition of the active practice of law. However, he does like meeting people. At that time he proposed setting up a loan business as a sideline and I encouraged him. It developed so rapidly within the next three years that almost all of his time is now spent in the loan business, and his income from it is double that of his best year in the practice of law. And he has built up the servicing of accounts which, like a life insurance agent's renewal commissions, could constitute a substantial source of income for future years.

One business leads to the other

If the real estate agent is also a general insurance agent, he will have many opportunities to write fire, liability, and other coverages upon property which he manages or sells. The two businesses dovetail together, each increasing the possibilities of the other. For example, if one calls upon lawyers for real estate listings, the same discussion may bring up the subject of fidelity or procedural bonds. One calling upon an insurance prospect may find that he wants to sell a house, and thus may obtain the listing of such property.

A general insurance agency in a good location often can be developed within a comparatively few years to the point where it returns a very adequate income. Since much of the business thereafter consists of renewals, I have known of cases where the agent has devoted his time largely to other enterprises after establishment, yet, received a substantial annual income by having a well-trained office girl, plus, perhaps, one male employee to call upon new prospects. At any rate, this is a type of business which is profitable when properly operated, and which requires no great outlay of capital.

Build a clientele

One of the quick ways of building up a clientele is to buy the business of older agents, retaining such accounts and adding to them. Sometimes these persons want to retire and to get ride of the headaches attendant upon servicing the policy contracts; occasionally, the companies which they represent put on pressure to require them to transfer their accounts to a younger, more vigorous, man. One may acquire several of such accounts as a nucleus of an agency business. Often the purchase price, where fire and related policies are concerned, will run the amount of one year's average net income to the agent. Automobile and other liability coverages, because of the greater turnover, will be worth less and should be purchased more cheaply.

Any progressive agent will be alert to large premium risks, such as fleet coverages, insurance upon manufacturing plants or large stores, and enterprises where the opportunities for large commissions make it worthwhile to spend the time necessary to develop interest and to close the sale. Large bond risks are also well worthwhile. Of course, in life insurance, it may be necessary to represent one company alone and to concentrate upon that single activity. There is practically no money in so-called industrial or small premium policies, at least not for the agent.

Selling life insurance

In life insurance, it pays to concentrate upon professional and business men, or upon other persons of fairly substantial income. One can sell such insurance in blocks from $10,000 to $100,000 in the same time that it takes to sell a smaller policy to the average workingman, the policy is less likely to be lapsed, it may lead to future business from that individual or his friends, and it, of course, pays a much better commission. Group health and accident policies, insurance to fund trusts, and bonus or pension plans are extremely lucrative. And sales of health and accident policies help to meet current expenses. Of course, one's career may lead into executive employment by a single company with excellent opportunities.

At the moment, I am thinking of two ex-football players who quickly became members of the Million Dollar Roundtable which automatically means that their earned incomes are excellent. Bob Castelo and Ruck Steger are not, however, ordinary individuals. Bob Castelo is a Phi Beta Kappa, although he tries to keep that fact quiet. Ruck Steger is a person of unusual charm, who has a tremendous faculty for getting along with people. Both have planned exactly where their particular markets are, where they can render a genuine service, and bear the best interests of their clients in mind when making their proposals. Success has followed, of course.

Ideas are always needed in advertising

Another field of profitable personal endeavor is that of advertising. There are not too many creative idea men, which fact helps to make one who is talented in this direction valuable both to industry and to advertising agencies. One of my favorite stories is of the cannery unable to sell a large shipment of white salmon, housewives being accustomed to pink or red salmon. Taking their problem to an advertising man, he changed the loss into a quickly realized profit merely by adding these words to the label: "Guaranteed not to turn pink in the can."

There are thousands of apt examples to illustrate the important role of practical advertising. Some advertisements breed resentment, so that the reader or listener vows never to buy that particular product. Advertising based upon lies or false premises may convince momentarily, but the adverse reaction thereafter is terrific. The same is normally true of repetitive advertising—it may capture attention, but in a negative manner. Good, convincing advertising based upon some honest sales point is always sound. And humorous advertising—which is no good unless it's very good—may serve to impress the name of the product upon the customer's mind permanently.

But one does not have to deal in advertising as a livelihood in order to profit by its lessons. You'll find it pays to look at your product through the eyes of the copywriter who has to ask himself: How is the product made? Can it be made better, stronger or cheaper? Can it be made streamlined or more attractive? Can it be better packaged for eye appeal? How are we going to market it, and can we go a better way?

And with a service: How is it presented to the prospective user? Is it being professionally handled? Can it be made better, more modern, in any way more effective?

Above all—how does my product or service compare with other products or services being offered around town?

PRACTICAL POINTERS

1. There is great opportunity in the professions. Become aware, however, of how a professional man must prepare and how his profession shapes his life.
2. To succeed in a profession, be businesslike. Once again, the good manager is a valuable man.
3. In the tremendous field of selling, you may make more money with less preparation. And you probably can sell better than you think. Salesmen always are needed and they can make money in good times and bad.

8

Getting into Insurance,
Banking or Finance

NOT TOO MANY of my readers will establish such major enterprises as an insurance company, a bank or a finance company.
But most of my readers are likely to deal with such organizations; in fact, you hardly can escape it. It pays, therefore, to
know what goes on inside the organizations that handle so
much of our money. And certainly many of us will invest
our dollars in one way or another and with such organizations. At the very least, a little study may help an investor to
have some idea of why some such businesses flourish like the
"green bay tree" while others stagnate or wither.

Know the "musts"

Many persons have attained wealth from the establishment of insurance companies. There are five chief factors
which determine whether or not the entrepreneur will attain

success: (1) a well-conceived agency plan with possibilities
for rapid mushrooming; (2) sound underwriting; (3) sound
claim and legal policies; (4) sound actuarial planning; (5) a
central agency plan from which the idea man can realize
either income or capital gain. Investment aspects are not
placed in this "must" category since, with strict statutory and department regulation of insurance companies, any
sound investment man cannot go too far astray.

Taking agency as the first step, the companies which have
shown the most rapid growth in recent years, so far as liability policies are concerned, are those built around such integrated units as farm bureaus. The State Farm Mutual
Automobile Insurance Company, for example, in slightly
over 30 years developed from a gleam in George Mecherle's
eye to a company having in excess of half a billion dollars in
annual premium income. The Nationwide, formerly the
Farm Bureau Mutual, of Columbus, Ohio, the Farmers Insurance Exchange of Los Angeles, the Country Mutual Insurance Company, and other companies have grown to
tremendous size using somewhat similar nuclei. Yet, there is
certainly no reason why farmers should be considered as the
ideal hub for an expanding business. In the instance of the
State Farm Mutual, for example, farmers constitute only a
moderate portion of its policyholders; the other business
upon its books has been developed in more normal patterns
using conventional selling methods except, however, operating as a direct writing company. This prevents the appoint-
ment of agents who might, in the event of dissension, switch
the business so carried to another company.

The Allstate Insurance Company, springing from the ro-
bust loins of Sears, Roebuck, is making a phenomenal
growth. Automobile insurance is scarcely figured as mail
order business, yet Allstate is an example which proves how
wrong average concepts can be. Of course, local offices have
been established for that organization, just as Sears has established retail outlets throughout the nation.

One of the important things to remember is that the sole

purpose of insurance is to meet an existing need. In order to outpace competition, a young company must study as to where a "void" in protection exists, then design a contract to fill that void. Resourcefulness of that kind, aggressively marketed and adequately reinsured, can spell success.

Good risks and bad risks

There are many groups which could constitute a nucleus around which to build an agency business for, let us say, an automobile insurance company. What about professional men? Physicians? No! They drive under all road conditions, at all hours of the night, when fatigued and under strain. Lawyers? Probably yes. Their risks are less hazardous. Engineers, architects, and accountants normally would be sound risks.

School teachers and university professors present large groups of potentially desirable, yet largely unorganized, policyholders who might well be so handled. Labor unions would suggest mass potential groups of policyholders upon a non-selective basis. Ministerial associations could be among the better risks. And perhaps insurance companies could be worked through particular church organizations and bear such a name, even as the term "Lutheran" is reflected in the title of a present company.

If this were done, one could, perhaps, use persons already active in such organizations in creating the nucleus for an agency force. In fact, there is no reason why several different companies could not be initiated by the same founder, each bearing some title attractive to the particular group, yet consolidating the investment, underwriting, and claims departments for a reduction in cost operations—maintaining separate reserves and expense factors. Each company could contract with the parent organization to handle these functions for a percentage of the gross premiums, yet acting under close supervision of the State Departments to be certain that no abuse would arise.

In underwriting, the test usually is that of selectivity. A company can progress only so long as it is competitive. It must, therefore, weed out poor risks before they have an opportunity to affect loss ratios detrimentally. In automobile insurance, for example, one must weed out the very young and the very old driver, the drunkard, the accident-prone person, and the person of poor repute. In this endeavor, he is somewhat handicapped in that the State Departments have an assigned risk plan under which they compel insurance companies to insure the bad driver upon some type of allocation basis. Obviously, the very bad driver should be taken off the highways, instead of being permitted to continue to drive and to kill others.

Why companies go broke

An illustration of why insurance companies go broke is given by a company that was organized in this community several years ago. It was administered by executives who knew little about insurance company operations. It was the conception of these persons that all they had to do was to get business on the books, and that such business would automatically take care of any future problems. The company secured business very quickly, because it is a simple matter to get a volume of bad business. The rates were not actuarily computed, a multitude of bad risks were accepted, no sound underwriting practices were followed, and the company was shortly insolvent. Similarly, it is easy to secure long haul truck insurance business, but few companies have made a profit in writing that type of risk. It takes a person with special capacities, who knows that type of business thoroughly, to handle it properly.

In other types of insurance, such as in life, health, and accident insurance, an adequate medical history and thorough physical examination may be of the greatest value. In certain types of such insurance, such as business written through groups or associations, underwriting may be waived.

Normally, where policies are individually written, however, one of the most important factors is the integrity and capability of the agent himself, who knows much about the person he solicits, and who acts in reality as an underwriter in the field.

The actuary should call the tune

All insurance companies require good actuarial guidance. Actuaries, in considering underwriting factors and experience, determine the premium rate to be charged. In life insurance, the mortality rate is quite uniformly favorable and this immediately would seem to be the most profitable field of insurance. This has proven true in viewing those stocks as investments, as compared with the stocks of other insurance companies. However, there are factors which can militate against the success of even such an operation. The premium rate, once fixed on a life insurance policy, is constant; in the event of an epidemic or of a nationwide casualty, such rate cannot be readjusted. The decline in investment rates and difficulties in finding investments may present other problems. Liability policies and property coverages may show a higher average loss ratio and expense of adjustment items; they may fluctuate more grossly; but the policies are short-lived and thus may be readjusted more easily as to premium charge.

The claim and legal departments can either make or break an insurance company. One of the largest factors in adverse loss ratios is penury in claim administration. Wise claim policy requires competent travelling adjusters, sufficient in number to handle claims within 48 hours of the time they arise. If a claim is presented in an area where a travelling adjuster is not conveniently available, competent independent adjusters can be secured. Sound claim policy requires quick and sometimes liberal settlements. Overpayments upon cases may impoverish a company. However, almost without fail, it is the company which chronically denies claims or is niggardly in approaching the matter of settlement which has a tremendous number of cases in litigation. And it is those companies which, as the expression goes in the trade, "have their loss ratios catch up with them" and often go into receivership. Any young company must, of course, reinsure the vast bulk of its business until it sheds its swaddling clothes.

The central agency plan

It has often been asked as to how any insurance company can produce sums of money to a founder, in view of the fact that such companies are largely owned by policyholders or, as in a mutual company, by members. In this regard, one must be familiar with the operation of a central agency plan, or management company. The central agency or management company, in which the founder is usually the chief shareholder, contracts with the insurance company either to handle the writing of all its policies, or to perform certain other functions, for a percentage of premium income. Membership fees may sometimes be charged, of which a percentage may also go to the central organization. If it operates as a true agency company, the agents in the field are often, then, employees of the central agency which retains a net portion of each premium collected. If the business expands into multimillion dollar brackets, even a modest percentage can be quite substantial. In these instances, the incentive occasionally is in the direction of increase in size, sometimes at the sacrifice of sound underwriting principles.

Banking as a business

The banking business has many things in common with the insurance business. Such institutions are quasi-public in nature and closely regulated by a public department. A banking corporation must, accordingly, be organized under particular state banking laws, or under the applicable Federal statutes, where organized as a national bank. Because of the wide variation in and complexity of the laws which apply, no effort will be made to discuss those institutions in any great detail.

The important thing in the establishment of a bank is to have sound personnel. This requires persons of integrity, who are well-liked in the community, who know the banking business thoroughly, and who are sensitive to current banking needs and practices. For example, in Champaign, the founder of one bank was a person who invested substantially all deposits in United States government bonds. No one could quarrel with the safety of the organization, but it was not a commercial bank, as that term is used in modern parlance.

That bank has since been taken over by a group of progressive businessmen who have established a completely different type of institution. A new banking building has been erected in an area which gives ample room for parking and for drive-in facilities. The atmosphere of segregation of the officers and tellers from the customers has been abandoned in favor of a cordial but business-like atmosphere. New personnel has been introduced into the bank and competent older personnel retained, aware of the needs in commerce and industry, and as a result this bank is now an active force in the business life of this community.

The personal touch

Banks have come to realize that they have a function to serve which is more than merely offering a man an umbrella when the sun shines and taking it away when it rains. It is necessary for a bank to have a closely integrated relationship with its depositors, and to fill their day-to-day needs. Thus, the modern banking institution is trying to get its depositors to know its officers as individuals, and to come to their banker in time of need. Thus, facilities are now offered in the financing of automobiles, in the making of small loans, and in the solving of other financial problems which arise from time to time. More and more, such institutions are rendering a valuable service as administrators or executors of estates, as trustees of living or testamentary trusts, and as conservators of spendthrift or other estates.

Where such an institution is formed, and conducted in accordance with modern banking principles, it can be an excellent investment. In the first place, there is the income received from loans which the bank makes. There is an income from investment and government securities. There is the income from service charges, trustees' fees, and other services. Any modern, progressive institution can substantially increase its revenues by the use of those auxiliary services.

Investment businesses may be either wholly in the nature of personal service businesses—those which employ both personal and borrowed capital, such as small loan or automobile finance businesses; or those which deal wholly with customer capital, such as investment syndicates. And, in addition, there are those who deal as experts or counselors with the public.

The investment dealer

Such as an investment broker depends upon the skill and integrity of the individual, his reputation among clients, and his contacts with major brokerage houses and underwriters. Since it is almost wholly a commission type of business, income may vary widely from depression years to years of prosperity. Unless one develops a tremendous volume of transactions, the gross return is no more satisfactory than that of other personal service businesses.

On the other hand, investment syndicates and investment trusts are now just beginning to come into their own. Few private investors have sufficient capital to secure an adequate spread for safety—yet they are reluctant to secure only a low interest rate from government bonds, which increase is itself consumed by continuing devaluation of the dollar. The individual wants a larger yield upon his investment and some possibility of appreciation in value in times of prosperity. He may be able to buy a few shares of General Motors, A.T. & T. or some other stock, but he cannot carry a balanced program by himself. Pension plan funds, bonus trust funds, and other funded plans which are small in size have a similar problem.

How an investment syndicate works

Investment syndicates permit one to purchase a share in a business the entire assets of which consist of the holdings of public corporate bonds and the capital stock and bonds of private corporations. In a well-managed syndicate, such securities are spread wisely among so-called "gilt edged" and more speculative securities, in an attempt to balance factors of safety, yield, and appreciation in value. Some plans are devised so that the investor can purchase into one of several categories of securities—industrials, rails, bank stocks, oil stocks, life insurance stocks, growth stocks, etc. Under some plans the investor may invest twenty-five or fifty dollars every month which is included with like funds of others for periodic investment.

Such investment syndicates and mutual fund shares are growing by leaps and bounds. New organizations have been started within the last few years and are doing well, as should any such company when the stock market is travelling in only one direction.

★   *It has long seemed to me that a real need exists for a private investment trust to be called "Opportunities, Inc.," or some such title. This organization would use the funds of investors solely for the purpose of buying bargains—such as real estate offered at a sacrifice through an estate, large blocks of stock purchased from estates or receiverships at less than market value, and the thousand and one opportunities that arise daily but which an individual with limited finances cannot personally handle. The right man at the head of such an organization, who is cautious and shrewd, but quick to recognize a bargain and to act promptly, and who develops the proper contacts for information, and who travels from place to place to secure excellent deals could make both himself and members of such a syndicate wealthy.*

Building and loan companies

Building and loan, or savings and loan, institutions are pretty widely established now and are highly competitive. Here, there is a possibility of value enhancement arising from the spread between interest paid to depositors or members and that received from outstanding loans. Upon a twenty-million dollar deposit total, this spread would amount to several hundred thousand dollars, not including the income from service charges and discounts.

Small loans can be a bonanza

A different situation exists with reference to the small loan and automobile finance businesses. The day is past when the lender can charge 100% upon a six-month loan, but the odds are still greatly in his favor. The automobile finance company, for example, charges a flat handling charge by discounting upon a basis of, let us say, six per cent per year upon the initial gross balance over the life of the instrument. Upon a $1,200 deal, then, with a one year repayment, it receives $72 immediately, which is its gross return from that loan, not counting insurance commissions, etc. It borrows the money from a bank, paying a lower rate of interest for the use of the money, and has the security of the conditional sales contract and insurance policy to indemnify it against loss. Upon wholesale floor plans, however, different problems are presented—and a finance man must be extra vigilant if he is to avoid loss at the hands of sharp-shooting automobile dealers. A smart, tough man can get rich on wholesale financing transactions; an easy-going, nice kind of a guy will lose his shirt in a hurry.

My wife, Jean, got a liberal education a few years ago into what collateral charges in the purchase of an automobile can run. She priced a little Chevrolet Impala, which had been repossessed after being driven 3,000 miles, and was shown the original invoice. With all of the gingerbread and trimmings, the original basic invoice price was approximately $3,840. With automobile cost, handling charges, insurance charges, and other items based on a 30 month repayment, it came to a little over $5,100. Imagine, $5,100 for a Chevrolet! Then, for the first time, she realized how much of a differential there can be between paying cash and financing in this manner. (Yes, to answer your question, she did buy it for cash at $1,000 off the original invoice price, or $2,840.)

Small loan businesses resemble more closely the individual car financing operation. Usually no discount device is employed. But the finance company borrows the money from a bank at 4% to 4¼% interest per annum which it loans, depending upon the amount involved, usually at 1½% to 3% per month. The ratio of losses is small in a well operated company, and the profit is proportionately large. Such companies can be developed upon a chain basis in a comparatively short period and, with competent personnel, may expand to a position of importance in the financial world. However, whereas it is the popular conception that the small loan person is a callous individual, indifferent to the plight of those who borrow from him, most individuals and companies which attain success in that enterprise are responsive to the needs of those with whom they deal, and they are considerate of their economic situations if disaster strikes.

(When we come to family finances we shall look at the other side of borrowing money.)

A fascinating but specialized loan service

One of the fascinating personal businesses is that of bail bonds. Professional bondsmen generally own a dozen or so dilapidated pieces of real estate. These persons either hang around courthouses, or have friends in the sheriff's office who call them when persons are picked up charged with crime. These same deputy sheriffs or policemen (who may receive a slight token of esteem) give the bondsman information about the individual, and the bondsman does some personal checking, so that he may determine whether the bond would be safe. Generally, he takes a note and indemnifying agreement from relatives to protect him against loss, places himself upon the bond, and collects a substantial fee. I have never known a smart bondsman to go broke, and I have known of many attaining wealth.

PRACTICAL POINTERS

1. Insurance companies must be run on a strictly actuarial basis. Also the claims and legal department can make or break an insurance company. Good companies show great growth.
2. Banking is important for the business of any community. A bank can render many services, and a bank that is well-run on modern principles becomes a friend of those who deal with it.
3. Money borrowed from a bank at moderate interest can be re-loaned in various ways at higher interest. On this plan many loan companies and chains of loan companies are founded.

9

Manufacturing—on Any Scale

MANUFACTURING, despite its thousand headaches, does offer a road to financial success. Many of us may have the vision of machines clanking away, or of workmen at benches or assembly lines, turning out something large or something small that people want. The vision is sound . . . provided the thing you make is well made, reasonably priced and has a market.

Manufacturing can be a big business or small one, or anywhere in between. As we shall see, a big business almost always requires a number of small businesses to cater to it—and the small firms can get along quite well. The factor of labor relations becomes very important if one goes into manufacturing; it's a huge subject, of course, and I shall touch upon it only briefly.

Some thirty years ago, when I was taking a census for a city directory, I stepped into a ramshackle little building near the railroad. I found a number of people busy over machines that were making—to my surprise—nothing but tacks. But the product was good, the market was wide, and the man who owned the business made a respectable amount of money. The same individual probably could do well in almost any other phase of manufacturing. Basic principles are the same; it is only the degree of technical knowledge pertaining to the particular product or techniques, or the particular market, which varies.

A time to save and a time to spend

It is necessary that substantial sums of money be taken in, and that there be a respectable profit margin in proportion to the gross business transacted. Accordingly, one must concentrate primarily upon cost and expense factors if that margin is to be maintained. He must learn how to avail himself of discounts upon materials secured, how to buy his supplies at the lowest possible cost, the most economical methods of attaining maximum production, and the reduction of expense in every way which counts—which may mean, however, keeping efficiency high by payment of adequate wages.

Usually the successful manufacturer is a man who has learned his way from the bottom—worked as janitor, shipping clerk, office boy, bookkeeper, production man—one who undersands all phases of the business, the complaints of labor, and the problems of management. Sam Auerbach, a onetime employer of mine, told me that there was no phase of the trousers manufacturing business at which he had not worked, and that for some years he worked twice the number of hours of any employee, because it was his task to do all the jobs which he could not afford to pay others to do. The ideal background is for one to have worked summers while in high school and college at each operation of a particular manufacturing business, while young and unprejudiced and before the workmen don the protective armor of aloofness worn against college graduates; then to have majored in business engineering and administration; and finally to have had some substantial experience under the guidance of production experts.

Walter Chrysler spoke of the completion of the great Chrysler Building in New York City, and of a conversation he had with his son at that time. He said:

> "When he was ready to go to work, I said, 'You better learn something about the building. It's yours; not mine.'
> " 'Where do you think I ought to begin, Dad?'
> " 'Get down in the basement and learn what the other fellow's got to do. Go and scrub a few floors. Clean some offices. That way you can begin to see through the glasses of other people as well as your own.' He did it, too, and then proceeded through various jobs until he was well able to run the building. That enterprise is working now as in 1929 it was planned that it should." *

Henry Peterson, of Feature Ring, was his own engraver, errand boy, janitor, and jack-of-all-trades, working until 2 A.M. including Saturdays and Sundays.† He feels, however, in his own case that he carried this to an extreme. Nevertheless, one entering that field must do so not with an "executive complex," but with humility, a fierce desire to succeed, and a willingness to work as hard as necessary in achieving that objective.

Manufacturing is often a short-cut to wealth, if the product is new and revolutionary or fills a long felt need. And it is true that, given management experience, the first thing to determine is where a need exists which is not being satisfactorily filled under present competitive conditions. In some phases of industry, competition is sufficiently keen, or the capital required is so enormous, such as in the automobile business, that a new business finds it difficult to establish an entering wedge. In other fields, incompetence may be more prevalent, or new techniques can be devised to reduce costs, so that a well-managed new industry can succeed. And, of

* *Life of an American Workman,* p. 199.
† *Operation Success,* p. 164.

course, if a business acquires a good, new type of product not of the gadget variety, it may create its own market.

The difficulty with many young industries, however, is that they may permit themselves to become wholly dependent upon a single outlet such as a chain store or mail order house and thereafter remain at its mercy. A well-diversified group of customers is much to be preferred.

Big business needs small business

It was pointed out in an excellent article by Albert Nickerson, vice-president of the Socony Mobil Oil Company,* that there are many markets to be filled by small business handling items which the big corporation cannot manufacture efficiently or deal with in any reasonable manner. His expression is particularly appropriate, when he states:

> "Of course, the giants don't do business with the midgets out of charity or sentiment. They freely admit that there are essential jobs for which a big company is no more suited than a sledgehammer for swatting flies."

Each year, his own company pays out nearly $450,000,-000 to 30,000 small companies. Their services include landscape gardening, lock maintenance, carpeting, packaging of box lunches, asphalt, salvaging of scrap metal, and many other industries which fill needs which the bigger corporation had neglected. Wherever a need exists, a successful enterprise can be created.

If one enters the business of manufacturing—let us say, a new appliance or device—he must remember that his capital must be sufficent for his needs. It takes about two years to put a new machine over. In addition to the pattern-making, designing, and actual manufacture of any item, one has to sell the distributor upon taking on the new item. The dis-

* "How Big Business Hatches Small Business," *Coronet*, June, 1958, p. 127.

tributor has to sell the dealer, and the dealer must sell the customer. By the time it all produces results in the factory, two years may have elapsed.*

Check yourself right down the line

There are some matters to which any manufacturer should give particular attention. One is the danger of overestimating what his business will be and overpurchasing supplies. In the first place, capital which is tied up in raw material is not working, it is not earning money, and, most important, it is not available for other needs. Enough supplies should be available to fill current and immediately anticipated needs, and sometimes substantial purchasing may have to be done against the danger of a sharply rising market price. But overpurchasing, where there is a sudden stoppage of orders, can break even a well-established company.

Another thing which must be remembered in any business is to take care of orders and correspondence immediately, without delay. It has long been a habit of mine to dictate a reply to each letter the same day it is received, if I am in town. I know that I personally resent having to wait a week or more for a reply to my own communications, and this necessarily affects my evaluation of my correspondent. As Max Hugel pointed out, "Delay an answer and a customer can change his mind or talk to a competitor." †

A third thing which any manufacturer or other businessman must keep in mind is that the morale of his plant must be kept at a high level. There is one major automobile manufacturer which had a protracted strike and labor difficulties. For at least a year after that time, as an attorney, I came into contact with dozens of instances where parts of the auomobile simply fell off, because of shoddy workmanship. I even ran into situations where workmen had stuffed the remnants of their lunches in the body of the car, ap-

* *Operation Success,* p. 141.
† *Ibid.,* p. 139.

parently thinking it was cute. As a result, much good will was lost, hurting them as well as their employer. The manufacturer must also take advantage of discounts. The discount percentage may equal in size the net profit from product sales. The supplier acts not only as a banker but makes it profitable for a marginal enterprise to operate in the black.

Fourth, cut costs. There never was a business so well run that there was no waste in it—no places where time and money could not be saved. Except where it would be destructive to morale, the savings so effected can spell the difference between success and failure.

Geography counts

A person planning to go into manufacturing should be flexible in his thinking. For example, if he plans to handle subcontracts, normally he should operate close to prime contractors in order to hold down shipping costs and lost time. If he is an independent manufacturer, he must consider climate, power, labor supply, accessibility and cost of raw materials, accessibility to market, shipping costs of materials and finished product, and many other things.

Obviously, there are some advantages to certain southern climates over that in northern states. If heating costs in winter are reduced and the absence of snow and ice minimizes accidents and shipping slow-downs, certain cost factors may be reduced. Perhaps, also, labor works for a lower average rate in such communities and is more plentiful. On the other hand, excessive summer heat may reduce efficiency during those months, labor may be less skilled, and reduced health and sanitation facilities may increase absenteeism. These factors must be studied carefully and weighed against each other. Metropolitan areas offer a large supply of labor but, as opposed to this advantage, a greater competition for labor's services in periods of high production; and urban areas usually mean higher land costs, rental expenses, and construction costs.

★ *A person constructing a plant in Colorado may have cheap power, reducing production expense—but if his product is bulky or perishable, and his market is New York City, the saving may be turned into a large deficit. In such a case, the plant must be erected close to the market. There is no single solution to all problems; the answer must be evolved by weighing all considerations together. Only a careful study will suggest the answer.*

When to get started

There are two particularly good times to enter the manufacturing business. One is in the heart of a depression which is, incidentally, a good time to enter any business. While competitors are stuck with high-priced plants, costly inventories, and expensive raw materials, the new industry can get off to a flying start with a comparatively small investment. Then, when the upswing in industry arrives, it has a foot in the door and can expand rapidly. Therefore, its initial plans should be made wisely as to choice of location, ample room for expansion, etc.

The second time is during a period of national emergency. War contracts are easily available, or, even if not working upon war contracts, many other businesses are classified as essential. This affords an opportunity to do a great deal of building, to acquire needed machinery, and to depreciate plants and equipment at a five-year rate—thus winding up the emergency period with plants and equipment paid for out of tax moneys and several million dollars richer. Many men have made tremendous fortunes from securing government loans in the inception to build such plants, charging off the plants as stated, charging off the loan interest from taxable income, and repaying the loans from the cost-plus contracts.

It is impossible, of course, to discuss every element of

all types of major enterprises. It is felt, however, that the indication of a few of the leading types of businesses will suggest others to the reader—and an indication of some of the problems, which are often forgotten until disaster strikes, may save dollars and heartaches. Therefore, many of these principles discussed in connection with one type of enterprise should be recalled in considering others.

Some men specialize in taking over "sick" corporations. Some of these operate from a short term point of view, upon a purely selfish basis. For example, by slashing the salaries of key personnel, chopping off other employees, and cheapening a product, the profits may be made to appear to zoom during, let us say, a twelve-month period. An individual of this type may then boost the price of the stock, sell out, and quit. He misses the chaos which follows after him from the loss of such key individuals.

Others, however, fall in the role of business doctors, building up sound enterprises from those which were retarded, for one reason or another, and often combining corporations for the benefit which each of several different operations can bring to the other. These, then, have the makings of sound, permanent enterprises, and such entrepreneurs serve a valuable function in a society based upon private capital.

New directions in technology

In the United States today, our technology is moving in a new direction. In the last century, we had what could be called the "coal technology." We had coal-fired steam locomotives, coal-produced electrical power, coal-heated homes. In the last 50 years, we have seen primarily an "oil technology," with oil coming to be a more important source of fuel and power than coal. We are now in what is commonly called an "electronic and atomic era." And there is no question but that new sources of power, and new technologies, are developing rapidly.

Whenever this happens, it means that industry develops a completely new face—that new industries, heretofore unheard of, develop. New goals are set. Now we are talking in terms of outer space, of rockets, missiles, and space craft. Whenever a new technology develops, one entering that type of field encounters new and additional problems. There may be great rewards; however, there are also great risks and great demands upon venture capital. This is no place for the ignorant. We are seeing, and will see in greater measure in years to come, the emergence of the scientist businessman; a picture in which the stereotyped ingenuous chemist or engineer emerges into an individual knowledgeable both in the technical and financial aspects of his industry.

PRACTICAL POINTERS

1. In manufacturing above all, it pays the owner of the business to know every part of and how every job is done.
2. You don't have to be big to make money. Just be sure your product has a market, even if the market is a bigger company.
3. Times of depression and times of national emergency are good times in which to get started as a manufacturer.
4. Industry will grow as America grows, by keeping attuned to its changing needs; those who would prosper must grow in knowledge and aptitudes with the changing pattern.

10

How to Finance a Business Enterprise

THE BUSINESS OF FINANCE may seem to be very complicated. It is not, in fact, the simplest matter in the world, but it is certainly understandable. This understanding is very important. First, any person who plans to enter any kind of business—unless he already has all the money he needs—must understand the rules of financing, and how they operate in his own situation, or he'll never get off the ground. Second, you must understand these basic principles before you can invest wisely in someone else's business.

As you will see, a good part of this chapter is reminiscent of the chapter on the Stock Market; but it carries matters quite a large step further. Here, too, we see how the law limits you when you issue stock, how partnerships, joint ventures and associations are set up, and how corporations come into being and do business.

This is followed by a description of the several types of

securities that may be issued, and a discussion of short-term credit. By then you will have seen how cautious you must be when you ask other people to trust you with their money—and how well it pays to have any enterprise fully and soundly financed.

Let us assume Joe Brown wants to start a shoe store. He needs money to rent the premises, to buy inventory, to furnish the place, to buy equipment, to pay insurance and utilities, to advertise in the paper, and possibly to pay for some help in the store.

The first thing that I would tell every Joe Brown is that there are two pieces of property he should never touch for any business venture, since there is always a fair possibility of failure. First, he should never put a mortgage upon his house for this purpose. There may already be a mortgage upon the house; that is all right, but if the house is not encumbered, it should not be mortgaged for the purpose of a business risk. The second thing is that a man should not borrow upon his life insurance for this purpose. He could be jeopardizing the security of his family if he did so; in addition, the time may come when a few hundred dollars will make the difference between staying in business and failing, and there is that cushion which one could, in time of an emergency, fall back upon.

Put it in writing, in legal terms

So Joe borrows $1,000 from Aunt Minnie, $500 from Uncle Walter, and $3,000 from six of his lodge brothers. He promises each of them that he will cut them in for a piece of the profits, when he starts making money. The first thing Joe needs right now is a good lawyer—and I would say that Aunt Minnie, Uncle Walter, and the six friends need to talk to one also. This lawyer will insist that the details of the borrowings be put down in black and white, and that any advancement be represented by a written note, stating exactly what it provides, nothing more and nothing less. If Joe is, in effect, promising them shares in the business, or is limiting repayment to be made solely out of profits, with a bonus if he proceeds, he may be running afoul of the Blue Sky Laws.

What is a Blue Sky Law? It sounds very pretty, but awfully technical. Well, in simple terms, it is simply a state statute which forbids a person to solicit interests in any kind of business for money without registering the nature of the business in the office of the Securities Department in that state and having it first approved. Normally, there is a minimum number of people to be approached—sometimes 12 or 25, or a minimum amount of money involved, such as $25,000, before the statute applies.

But its purpose is a good one. If there were no such state limitation, the citizens could be plucked clean by enterprising but unscrupulous promoters setting up small ventures within a state, selling the stock, and then going out of business. That sort of thing happens often enough even with such a law; it would be much worse without it.

Just recently, a former real estate man in this county organized a corporation to develop a system for teaching while one slept, through the use of records with the sound transmitted under the pillow. He did not solicit stock. Instead, he borrowed money and represented the borrowings by notes, which provided the conditions of repayment. The state stopped his raising of the money and required him to return all of the funds which he had raised in this manner. And, as I will point out shortly, there may be penalties which apply to the violations of such law.

★   *It is better for the Joe Browns to start small, and not with a flourish; to raise all of the money they can from their own resources or upon their personal credit, and to repay it as quickly as possible. If one keeps plowing back the income of his business into that business, usually its growth will take care of itself.*

Do you want a partner?

Often people like Joe find some other man who wants to go into a like business at the same time. There are some advantages in sharing the responsibility for the running of the business and the sharing of the responsibility for the raising of capital. Any partnership agreement should, of course, be prepared by a good attorney. If both are equal partners, sharing in the general operations of the business, the partnership is usually called a general partnership. Each, then, is fully responsible for all of the debts and obligations of the business. If one man puts in only money, frequently he insists upon the agreement being a "limited partnership," in which his liability is limited to the loss of his initial investment.

Partnerships tend to have headaches. Generally, one man begins to feel that he is working harder than the other, or that the other partner is not pulling his weight for some reason. Their personalities or temperaments may clash; their wives may get into an argument; or a partnership may dissolve for any one of a hundred reasons. For that reason, it is usually better, if one can afford to do so, to own the business outright and to hire the help he needs.

The joint venture

Somewhat similar to the partnership is the joint venture. This is a situation where two or more people both contribute money to do a specific thing—such as to buy a portion of an oil royalty, or to lease a piece of land, or to buy up surplus merchandise for resale. Usually it is a single-shot transaction, and it is found more often in oil well transactions than in any other. A joint venture may avoid partnership liability for the acts of the other joint venturers; otherwise, it is essentially similar to a partnership. When that particular transaction has ended, the relationship ends, but they usually share the liabilities and profits of the enterprise, in equal proportions, or in such different proportions as their contract provides.

The syndicate

A syndicate is generally a joint venture which has a longer period of prospective operation, and normally involves a group of people acting together. A group getting together for the purpose of producing a play on Broadway would be considered a syndicate. Again, in purchasing an interest in an oil well, where it is planned that such operation will go on for a considerable period of time, a syndicate form may be used. For example, a few years ago, there were several of us who became interested in a mineral venture in Arizona. Seven of us each contributed funds in equal proportions thereby reducing the expenditure necessary on the part of any one person (correspondingly reducing the prospect of profits, of course, as well). The venture did not work out, so the proportionate loss to any one was small. Sometimes these syndicates operate through a manager or a trustee, but in some such situations where the enterprise corresponds in all other respects with a corporation, except in name, the government treats it as a corporation and it is taxed accordingly.

Dry-well trouble

I mentioned earlier that there are penalties for violating the Blue Sky Law. I repeat it because the Law is a great source of trouble for the unwary. Two years ago, for example, a man we will call Jim Nellis promoted a group for the purpose of drilling oil wells. I am sure that he acted in complete good faith in soliciting money from 25 people and using that money to acquire mineral leases and to drill the wells. Unfortunately for him, the wells were dry.

Now our Illinois law provides that the sale of fractional

undivided interests in oil leases to more than fifteen persons, or where the total money raised is in excess of $25,000, is controlled by the statute. And where a person fails to register, each person who invested money can sue the promoter to get his money back plus interest. So the way it works, for all practical purposes, is that if Jim Nellis had hit, they would have accepted the profits had there been any; when the venture failed, they promptly sued.

Now the way this operates in practice, is that the state may learn about the venture from a disgruntled investor. They investigate and find that Nellis has violated the statute. So they call him on the carpet, having the right to institute criminal proceedings which may carry a fine up to $5,000 under some provisions or $10,000 under others, with imprisonment in the county jail or penitentiary depending upon the nature of the violation. In addition, they send out a notice to each investor of the nature of the violation and informing such persons of his rights. Nellis has the right, within thirty days of the time such notice goes out, to repay the full amount to each investor, in which case they can no longer sue him individually; otherwise, he is liable for the attorneys' fees as well.

★   *So it does not pay to fool around with violations of the Blue Sky Law. I have even had attorneys consult me who had failed to realize that something which was not a corporation might still be regulated under those provisions. If one has any question, he can always check directly with the appropriate state office, describe exactly what he has in mind, and secure a ruling upon it.*

Associations

Before going to the general matter of corporations, which are the principal medium of investment, I would like to say a word about "associations." These are organizations frequently resembling partnerships, but usually with a type of management which has a good many of the aspects of the business corporation. Physicians occasionally have set up clinics under an association plan for the purpose of deriving certain advantages relating to pension plans otherwise available only through a corporate structure. However, where there are advantages, there are also disadvantages; and an association may be taxed under the Federal income tax laws as a corporation. This would cause a double tax, in substance, the first being a corporation tax and the second being a personal income tax upon the individual members of the association. Its usefulness ordinarily depends upon the problems presented, frequently increasing in value in proportion to clinic size.

Corporations

Going now to corporations, it is important that one not think of such organizations as mammoth in size. Joe Brown may incorporate his shoe store for a variety of reasons. In the first place, if Joe should go broke, then all he would lose would be his investment in the corporation. The investor in the corporation, unlike the sole proprietor or partner, does not have a full responsibility for obligations of the business. He and the corporation are two different entities, and the corporation may be liable for things for which he is not. It is no pleasure, of course, for any businessman to become insolvent; but it is a theory of our law that one who deals with a corporation does so knowingly and in sole reliance upon the assets of the corporation. Therefore, if the corporation should fail, the operator of that business may be able, in time, to surmount that loss and establish another and more profitable enterprise.

Granting, therefore, that a corporation may be either large or small, it is necessary for any corporation to be capitalized—or, in simple terms, to have money with which to operate. The fact is that most corporate enterprises are undercapitalized. The result is either: (1) that the corporation goes broke because of a lack of reserves; or (2) it gets into a distressed situation, where someone else slips in and takes over control, in return for putting up a comparatively small amount of money. We have seen how profitable this can be from the investor's side. Accordingly, it is necessary first to determine the capital needed in the beginning, plus the extra working capital which may become necessary to continue successful operations. It is then further necessary to conserve those funds, once received, for their proper purposes. One frequently finds the founders of a business developing an "executive complex," feeling the sudden importance of being corporation executives, being overly impressed by their capitalization, and spending such money for overly expensive buildings, or simply "living high on the hog."

Bricks and mortar don't pay bills; a Cadillac cannot type. Cash is necessary for the operation of any business. This the founder (whether one or many persons) must have at the least expense to the company and to the founder. And, by expense, we mean not only the expense of interest charges but the expense of surrendering parts of company control.

How a corporation raises money

When a corporation sets out to raise money, normally that money is divided into two parts: capital, and paid-in surplus. Let us say that a corporation raises $100,000 through selling stock. In a financial balance sheet, it would show as an "Asset" cash of $100,000; but under "Liabilities" it would show an offsetting debit in that amount. Now, obviously, a corporation has to spend some money in getting into operation. For some of the dollars it spends, it may acquire other assets, such as a building, equipment, or merchandise, which would keep the asset side of the picture up to the same level. But it has to spend for other things which would reduce the assets, such as rent, salaries, and travelling expenses. Since there may be a considerable period of time, in the beginning, when the outgo is much more than the income, the assets may be cut in half.

So, taking our little corporation, if the entire $100,000 under Liabilities was represented by capital stock, when the assets were later cut in half, we would say that our capital stock was "impaired" by 50%. That we don't want, and the state might make the corporation stop doing business. So, when the stock is sold, we normally would have a majority of the price paid allocated to surplus. Suppose, in this little corporation, that on the Liability side of the ledger, we have "Capital Stock $25,000; Paid-In Surplus $75,000." As much as $75,000, then, of the amount originally paid in could be used for necessary corporate business without impairing our original capital. That is the purpose of surplus. No organization can get off the ground without some working capital.

Now, to raise this working capital, the corporation must sell some type of securities. (And here we have the other side of the picture we saw in the chapter on the Stock Market.) The general ownership of a corporation is normally represented by common stock. That is the stock which represents what we call the "equity" or true ownership of the business. As the value of the business increases, the value of the stock increases, or vice versa. And that is ordinarily the type of stock which is sold. The corporation we have just referred to might start with $10 par stock, selling at the price of $40 per share, to get the $75,000 of paid-in surplus we mentioned as opposed to the $25,000 capitalization.

Knowing stocks and bonds

Preferred stock is simply a different type of stock which has both advantages and disadvantages in its ownership. The big disadvantage is that it ordinarily does not increase in value proportionately to increases in value of the common stock. The advantage is that usually a certain interest rate is guaranteed; and, in the event a corporation went into bankruptcy, the par value of the preferred stock would be paid out to its holders before the common stockholders would receive anything. Of course, to be frank, if a corporation becomes defunct, ordinarily neither the preferred shareholders nor the common stockholders receive anything.

A typical share of preferred stock might be $100 par, bearing 5% cumulative interest—or, in other words, paying a five-dollar dividend each year; except that if the corporation is unable to pay the dividend one year, the next year it owes $10, and so on until it is paid. Where cumulative dividends are provided, it is usually illegal to pay any dividends to the common stockholders until all dividends in arrears are paid to the preferred shareholders.

To make preferred stock more attractive to purchasers, it is often made "convertible." This means simply that the holder of a preferred share can trade it in and get a certain amount of common stock for each share of preferred which he has. In the little corporation we have discussed, if the preferred stock was originally sold at $100 a share, and each share of common stock at $40 a share, it would probably provide that the preferred shareholder could get two and a half shares of common stock for each share he holds of preferred. That makes the holding of preferred stock decidedly more attractive. But it is the exception, rather than the rule, to find such preferred stock to be convertible into shares of common.

There are several other types of securities which are used to raise money for corporation purposes. One is bonds, which are something like fractional pieces of a mortgage. The corporation takes either all of its properties, or a part of its properties, and places a mortgage upon it which is held by a trustee, or bondholders' group. A series of bonds is then issued representing the total of such mortgage and sold to different persons. Those bonds usually provide for a definite retirement date, and bear interest at a designated rate. In the event the corporation should become insolvent, the bondholders would have to be paid off out of such property before anything could be paid either to preferred shareholders or common stockholders. However, that is not quite as good as it sounds. In the first place, the bondholders do not share in the growth and development of the business, or in its prospective profits. Yet, the physical assets of that business generally have a very small resale value for any different purpose, if it should go broke.

Debentures are a type of bond. Both bonds and debentures will normally be retired out of a sinking fund created out of profits for that purpose. There is an income tax advantage to the corporation in issuing either debentures or bonds as against preferred stock. The interest payments made by the corporation upon either bonds or debentures are deductible as business expenses (provided the proportion is not too "thin"—in which case they actually are stock, and treated as such); but not the dividends paid upon preferred stock. Therefore, the trend in corporations is toward the type of securities possessing those income tax advantages. Occasionally, debentures are made convertible, so that they can share in rising values by being converted into shares of common stock, similar to the privilege given to convertible preferred stock.

Bearing in mind, accordingly, the types of securities which a corporation may issue to commence business, or to raise money later, there are definite mechanical problems in getting such securities sold.

First, the paperwork

Assume I set up the XYZ Corporation in the state of New York for the purpose of manufacturing ladies' girdles. I want to raise $500,000 capital, but I decide that I can get by with raising $250,000 now, and perhaps a greater amount later. Therefore, I decide to sell 10,000 shares of five-dollar par common stock at a price of $25 a share, so that I will wind up with a net capital of $50,000, with $200,000 of paid-in surplus—minus, however, and this is important, the cost of securing that money.

Now, before I can sell a single share of stock, I must set up my corporation in New York State (either as a domestic or "foreign" corporation). My attorney prepares the corporation papers showing an authorized capital of the amount just mentioned, but an initial capital to be issued of, let us say, $5,000, and I immediately purchase and acquire 200 shares of the stock. So we get our corporation papers on that basis. What next?

First, we must qualify the corporation with the New York Securities Department for the sale of those additional shares of stock. At the same time we do this, we also qualify it with the Securities & Exchange Commission, under what is called Regulation A, if we are going to sell in any state other than our "home" state. That refers to corporations having a capital to be sold of less than $300,000. The procedure is simpler and less technical than a full-scale registration, and this could be handled through the New York City office of the Securities & Exchange Commission.

Now each of these places charges me a fee, and I have to pay that high-priced lawyer who does the work for me before both of these bodies. But our papers are approved by both Departments. Are we then ready to sell?

In New York State, yes; next door, no. If we wanted to sell in New Jersey, we would have to qualify the shares in that state, or at least comply with its "fraud" statute. Similarly, if we wanted to sell shares in Ohio, Illinois, or California, we would have to qualify those shares, or in other words register them with the appropriate Securities Department and get them approved, paying the necessary state fees, before we could transact that type of business there. So, let us say that we decide to limit our sale to three states, and qualify the issues in those states.

To get the approval of the Securities & Exchange Commission, we had to prepare and file a prospectus, which is an innocuous and rather unappealing document, warning everyone in effect that our securities are highly speculative and that they shouldn't touch them with a ten-foot pole. We had some printing expenses to pay, by the way, in that. So we decide we want to run a newspaper advertisement, or mail out a letter, which is much more glowing about our new shares. Can we do so? Uh, uh! Not without clearing it with the Securities & Exchange Commission, and it is highly unlikely that anything of a palatable nature will be approved.

Now our stock will not sell itself. Either we will have to get an underwriter, so-called, to sell the stock upon a commission basis, peddle it ourselves, or hire stock salesmen to do so. In any event, any person who is not registered as a licensed dealer in securities, or as a licensed salesman of securities, must then be registered in any state where he is going to sell. Sometimes this requires examination, other times it does not. But whoever undertakes to sell the securities must be licensed or the sales may be disapproved, and the money required to be refunded. Let us assume that the salesman, or underwriter, charges a 10% commission. By the time we have added up the commissions, the legal fees, the state and Federal fees, the revenue stamps which will be required on the stock certificates, the printing costs of the prospectus, and other expenses, we will probably find that our cost of getting the stock sold amounts to about 15%, and the entire stock issue may not sell.

★   *It is apparent from this that any person who figures on going into a corporate enterprise, and to raise the money from that to conduct his business, may have a delay of a year or more before he can get into operation. He must time his actions accordingly.*

Now, if I had decided to raise the entire $500,000 immediately, since that is in excess of the $300,000 limit under Regulation A, this would call for a full-scale registration in Washington, which generally causes even more delay, somewhat greater expense, and definitely greater scrutiny. If I have raised my entire $250,000 in the beginning through the stock issue, I may decide to use debentures for the second issue and qualify that under Regulation A, as well; and, since I then have a going concern, I may find these somewhat easier to sell.

Be sure you have enough

As I pointed out earlier, one of the great faults of the new enterprise is not securing sufficient capital initially. When this happens, it means that additional working capital must be secured. Two years ago, I saw a corporation in Wyoming which was really in trouble, because none of the persons at the head of it knew anything about corporate management or finance. Each time they wanted to pay a bill, or even pay wages, they simply issued more stock. The two things are grossly inconsistent. Capital stock is just what its name implies; it is long-term capital, intended to be permanent, issued for the purpose of creating the enterprise in the beginning, or of substantially expanding its operations later. Working capital, on the other hand, refers not to issues of such permanence, but to debentures, bank loans, and other sources of securing working funds. If the total capital is inadequate, then it should be increased, but not piece-meal.

Working capital may have to be raised to conduct business operations, if an adequate amount has not been earlier provided by paid-in surplus as we have discussed. Suppose, for example, one is in wholesale building materials. He may get in three carloads of material in one day, for which he has to pay immediately to secure his discounts. It may take him a month to sell those, and another month before he gets his money from the customers. Accordingly, he may be financing those enterprises for a period of sixty to ninety days. He knows he'll get his money eventually, with a profit, but in the meantime, he requires funds to carry those operations.

Getting a short-term loan

For purposes of that type, normally bank loans are available. That is the type of enterprise which the commercial banks were founded to handle. Ordinarily, short-term notes of sixty to ninety days are used. If the credit of the corporation is not good enough for an open or unsecured loan, then loans may be made upon the inventory or upon accounts receivable. In addition to banks, there are specialized houses which make loans upon accounts receivable or inventories. Loans may be made upon the basis of warehouse receipts, representing supplies or merchandise on hand, but not yet sold to third persons. Retail dealers in automobiles normally operate upon the basis of "floor plans," where the finance house advances the money necessary upon the basis of the average stock of automobiles carried, subject to adjustment upward or downward as the number of such automobiles increases or decreases. One may receive goods upon consignment, rather than being required to pay for them immediately. And, in more specialized operations, pledging and factoring may help to raise funds required for the business needs then existing.

Don't forget the other point of view

We have looked at this general situation primarily from the point of view of the person creating a business. In retrospect, then, we can analyze it from the point of view of the investor. It is apparent that ordinarily the new enterprise is speculative. Unless it is a type of business which offers great opportunities, and unless it has outstanding management, it is ordinarily well to avoid the new enterprise, with the many hazards which surround it, in favor of the time-tested corporation. Many new ventures never get off the ground—or, if they get off the ground, their fluttering wings may fail. But, if the prospects of that enterprise do seem excellent, then the investor wants to be an "equity" owner, or in other words, an owner of common stock. If he can give himself an extra safety valve, both as to income and preference in times of financial difficulty, through the means of convertible preferred stock or convertible debentures, that would be the most attractive means of investment. Otherwise, common stock would seem to be most desirable. Then would come regular bonds or preferred stock. But one who plans to invest in any enterprise should be familiar with the method by which it plans to operate, what its actual needs are at present, what they will be in the future, and what working capital will be available to it when once in operation. And any investor has a right to inquire about and to ascertain those matters before he cashes in his building and loan certificates to take a flier in a new company.

PRACTICAL POINTERS

1. Before you ask anyone to invest his money in your business, know your responsibilities.
2. Before you join in business with anyone, check all details with a lawyer.
3. Know the various forms under which a business can be organized, and which is right for you.
4. Issuing stock and selling it is not a simple matter. But it can be very advantageous.
5. Don't start a business in haste; make sure you are really ready.

11

Another Look at Service Enterprises

THE LONGER YOU'RE IN BUSINESS, the more you see it is pretty hard to put any business into a hard-and-fast category. A business may have elements of both service and selling, of manufacturing and distribution, or a combination of all these —with elements of both wholesale and retail operation.

In this chapter we'll look at various ventures that deal in service either almost entirely or to a large extent. Among others, we'll look into some of the problems of the retail outlet, parking lots and garages, beauty parlors. We'll briefly examine that very hectic business, running a grain elevator, as an example of special service to a special clientele. And we'll discuss the possibilities—and the dangers—of the more attractive of these opportunities.

★   *To run a retail outlet—whether you sell goods or service or both—you must be a man of many facets; an advertiser, skilled buyer, economist, prophet, executive and, of course, a salesman. Plus, naturally, a public relations man who has a very lively appreciation of the importance of good will.*

I read recently of a banker who had gone to prison and come out a wiser, sadder and completely poor man. But as he sat on a park bench in New York City, it occurred to him that thousands of people in the skyscrapers all around wanted to drink coffee in their offices, and a coffee-running business could be started with little or no investment. He hired hoboes to work for him on a percentage basis, and at first got his "coffee-and" from established lunch counters. Soon he rented a basement and ran a thriving business that, I believe, extended to complete box lunches. He was far from being the first in the business, in that locality, but he put a lot of drive into it and he got the trade.

The best place to sell complete box lunches is in an area of industrial or manufacturing plants, since the office worker is more likely to leave his premises at lunchtime. With this can go a candy and cigarette trade. Partial lunches or snacks often are well received at fraternities, rooming houses and dormitories in college communities.

Actual distribution of box lunches in a manufacturing area usually takes less than an hour immediately before and during the luncheon hours for each shift. Snacks in college towns have approximately a two-hour possible spread—from 8:30 P.M. to 10:30 P.M. The remaining work concerns itself with the preparation of the foods. After one has been in the business a few months, it is possible to estimate sales within five per cent accuracy or better, and the gross profit is high. In either case, quality must be good and appearance of the foods appetizing. It is suggested that an enterprising merchant should show a little cleverness in packaging the items, by novel recognition of holidays, current events, or other matters of interest to his customers.

A machine can do your selling

Along a similar line, the coin machine business (including candy, soft drinks, and cigarette vending machines, juke boxes, etc.) is at present rather good, particularly in busy locations. The amount of gross revenue necessarily depends upon the number of such machines in place, turnover per machine, service rendered, and expense of employees. The return for the amount of capital invested is substantial.

Another profitable type of business is that of the retailing of liquor—whether through taverns or package liquor stores. The price per drink served, of mixed drinks, is approximately eight times its cost. Package liquor stores operate upon a moderate margin, but the gross volume of sales per sales employee far exceeds that of comparable retail establishments. It is suggested that the most profitable type of package liquor store in the future will be the cut-rate, drive-in establishment which eliminates deliveries to customers completely and uses this saving, plus its large volume of business, to pass along reductions in price to the customer. A large establishment is not necessary—merely a store large enough to house the supplies attractively and adequate parking space. A man who does not make a 25% annual return upon his investment in a moderate- to large-sized community had better check up upon his employees. However, some states have civil liability statutes for persons engaged in that business, where injuries or losses are caused by intoxication. Insurance premiums are heavy, so that it may pay well to start in a non-statutory state.

Beauty at a price

Walk along any row of stores and sooner or later, probably sooner, you come to a beauty salon. It may be a simple, one-woman establishment—although the male hairdresser is often a valuable part of the scene—or it can range upward into a staff of a dozen or more skilled operators and equipment of all kinds.

The skill of the operator, of course, has everything to do with the success of the salon. And not only skill, but personality plays a big part here. Women would rather trust their hair, face and figure repairs to someone who glows with friendly confidence, rather than to someone of cold personality.

Larry Mathews, who established Beauty City in New York City, arranged his hair driers so that all the women sitting under the driers can watch the hair stylists at work. The driers are arranged in curved tiers, like seats in an auditorium. Not only does this keep women entertained while merely sitting, but it gives the stylists publicity and keeps them on their mettle.

Other features of this establishment show how beauty-servicing can be expanded. It has a beauty salon for children (start 'em young!) that provides free lollipops. There is also a health club with massage tables, showers, steam cabinets and other facilities. Patrons of the establishment also can secure light snacks, buy special cosmetics, accessories and even dresses.*

Up-grading

Often, a business succeeds better when its product or service costs more—provided a great sense of value goes along with what is sold. Some beauty salons and charm schools look like mansions—and milady seems quite willing to pay for the décor. An appeal to snobbery will often be carried over into certain other types of retail establishments, particularly such as dress shops, millinery stores, and jewelry stores. There, the cost factor may be the smallest deterrent to a purchase. The shop windows, in such event, would be reserved and dignified, price tags would not be in evidence, dress racks would be concealed, surroundings necessarily

* *Operation Success*, p. 192.

luxurious, and no charge would ever be made for incidental items, such as refitting or altering the lines of a dress or hat. The whims of an individual would be carefully noted down and remembered, such as a dislike for certain styles or colors. When buying trips are planned, the regular customer would be consulted as to particular needs and items would be purchased with that particular individual in mind.

Know your customers

There is no question but that appeals to snobbery are vast business producers with certain folks. You may have noticed how rapidly the appeal to snobbery has crept into television advertising of late. Instead of saying, "it will cost you less," more and more advertisers are saying; "it costs a few cents more, but you'll LOVE the difference." Or kindred phrases. The hint is there. We, the discriminating producer, are selling to you, the discriminating buyer.

On the other hand, such appeals discourage others. Jean and I would be a little embarrassed by those things, if too blatant. Furthermore, I like to look at price tags so I know in advance if I am going to be torpedoed. If mass sale is desired, then all thought of snobbery must be completely forgotten and the store must be conveniently located, friendly, and with commodities priced for maximum distribution. If quality is superlative, the price need not be strictly competitive, because people are ordinarily willing to pay for what they get. Excellent tailoring establishments, and indeed business ventures of all types as we have mentioned earlier, have created their own markets; and, here again, word of mouth advertising is frequently the difference between failure and success. Quality, above all, is important—quality of idea, quality of personnel, quality of merchandise, quality of service.

Parking: The unsolved problem

Parking lots and garages have immense potentialities. The rapid increase of retail stores and other "downtown" establishments with the corresponding increase in automobile traffic has created almost insurmountable parking problems in nearly every community. Parking problems have not been solved by parking meters. This solution has only partially alleviated the problem of the shopper. In no way has it solved the headaches of the person who drives his car to work. In large cities where the shopper is forbidden to park on downtown streets, he, or she, is in a like quandary; and even in smaller communities, the shopper must park at the fringes of the business area. It is very well to say that this problem is being solved by new enterprises going to the edge of communities where parking space is ample. But this is not accurate. The major businesses are still concentrated in a downtown area. They are not going to abandon their locations, buildings, or customers. Therefore, they must compete with new enterprises having parking facilities by providing a like service. How are they going to do it?

In small communities, parking lots municipally owned may be the answer. In larger cities, a different solution is required. Parking lots are wasteful of valuable space—accommodating 200 cars in an area which should accommodate 2,000. Obviously, then, cars must be parked underground or in the air. Storage garages are the only possible solution.

A municipal enterprise

A city can levy a bond issue to buy the ground and erect the building. It will lease the building to a private operator under an arrangement which will permit repayment of the bonds and interest within, let us say, a twenty-year period—with title to pass to the private owner when this occurs. In the meantime, ownership acquisition has been accelerated in the following manner: (1) No general taxes have been paid upon the structure during ownership by the city, considerably reducing overhead; (2) The lessee has been enabled to charge off from his annual income (if the contract was properly drawn) the amounts of his rental payments to the city. It, in turn, paid no income tax upon those receipts. The private owner will, upon receipt of title, convey it to a corporation paying, perhaps, a capital gains tax in order to permit the ultimate owner to set up an ample depreciation schedule.

I confidently predict that, within the next few years, entrepreneurs will start talking municipalities into going along with such plans, perhaps having an entire chain of many automobile storage buildings. The public, merchants, municipalities, and the entrepreneurs will all, in the long run, profit thereby. The loss of public revenue will be almost nothing in most cases during the interim period, since receipts would have been small prior to such construction—and, when public ownership has ended, the income taxes and property taxes will, in short order, more than make up an interim loss. This, I repeat, is one of the best possibilities of substantial gain presently existing.

A wheat-country special

Here in the Midwest we have a business that deserves anyone's attention as a sample of selling an important service —complete with headaches, plenty of risk, the possibility of disaster and the greater possibility of reward. I refer to running a grain elevator.

The money is made by buying from the farmer and reselling to the broker. For that operation, the elevator picks up several cents a bushel for acting as intermediary although it must, also, load the grain upon cars, arrange for transportation, etc. A like important aspect of such a business is the storage of grain for hire, which it receives during or following the harvesting season and, perhaps, stores during the winter for resale by the owner the following spring when prices may be higher.

If grain is accepted while too wet, it may build up heat causing spontaneous combustion or deterioration. The grain must be aerated and turned constantly, spot checks made of heat of the grain, and careful inspections taken to see that the grain does not deteriorate.

An elevator cannot afford to cheat, or discriminate against, a customer—or it will not long retain its following. On the other hand, it cannot stay in business long if it cheats itself. Its scales must be rigidly accurate, constantly checked. The loads brought in must be inspected to see that artificial weight does not affect the scale reading, and to determine moisture content and discounts accurately. In addition, the elevator operator cannot be so eager to obtain customers that he continually overextends himself upon credit to farmers or others trading with him.

On the other hand, it must be remembered that the grain elevator is the community center for a local trading area. The farmers and other customers expect to use the building as a meeting, and even a loafing, place. The operator cannot, therefore, act superior to his customers or he will shortly have no customers. He cannot isolate himself in a private office and ignore them, dress far superior to their attire, or put on airs which they may find offensive. He must give service, be friendly, extend reasonable credits, and retain both the respect and the liking of his customers. As in so many other service enterprises, the personality of the operator has much to do with success.

And while you're here . . .

Mike Menebree operated such a grain elevator. However, Mike realized that since the grain elevator was a community center that he could take advantage of its favorable position by making it a retail center, as well. Therefore, he stocked profitably dimensional and rough type lumber for farm construction, hardware, nails, paints, feeds, fertilizers, seed, farm implements, gasoline, and, in addition, he had some wholesale connections where other items could be ordered upon request, at a small markup. He more than doubled his income from ordinary elevator operations.

One trouble with such a business is the competition from consumer cooperatives, with tax discrimination in their favor. Another is that many grain operators sooner or later begin to believe that they can guess which way the market will jump. Sometimes they guess right the first few times, thereafter becoming bolder. If they guess wrong just once, they may lose the accumulated profits plus, perhaps, the business itself.

★   *There are many men who do not have the intestinal stamina to take a small certain profit and to ignore the large potential profits (or losses) which might result from speculation.*

On the other hand, storage warehouses are often highly profitable enterprises, particularly in areas where the rental or purchase cost of appropriate buildings with terminal facilities is not excessive. There is always substantial consumer demand. Frequently those businesses are operated in conjunction with moving and transfer lines. The first is a relatively safe, modest income business with good possibilities of permanency. The transfer business, like all transportation businesses, is highly competitive. The right man in any phase of transportation can grow rich in a comparatively few years—the wrong man, or even the right man with the wrong breaks, can lose his shirt so fast that he doesn't realize it is gone until he feels the breeze upon his bare back.

"The Aisle of Palms"

In speaking of motels, earlier in this work, I pointed out how much business they have taken from hotels. But hotels are very necessary in a city, and a good city hotel may make a lot of money. But it has big problems. There is the real estate investment to begin with; a suitable building in a good location. There is the staff, which can be considerable—both in the "front of the house," such as reservation clerks and bellhops, and the "back of the house" such as cooks and housekeepers. There are the many problems connected with catering to conventions and business shows, the holding of banquets and the like. A small-town hotel may be merely a somewhat extended rooming house. A big-town hotel becomes a city in itself, often containing shops enough to fill a small Main Street and offering every possible service from hat-cleaning to Turkish baths. The modern urban motel, of course, has like problems and like potential.

PRACTICAL POINTERS

1. A retail business requires the close personal attention of the proprietor and can stand or fall on his personality.
2. Parking is our great unsolved problem and it is getting worse. Look here for great opportunities to offer parking space and make money.
3. To succeed, make a plan and then follow through with all your courage and enthusiasm.

12

A Dollar for You, a Dollar
for Uncle Sam

IT MAY BE that a man who will cheat on his income tax return, when he is taxed half his profit, also would cheat if he were taxed a tenth of his profit.

Or it may be as former Commissioner of Internal Revenue, T. Coleman Andrews, once said: That our income tax laws have "the greatest potential that anyone has ever thought of for making out of us a nation of liars and cheats."

I believe our tax laws are doing great damage to our system of free enterprise. Be that as it may, I most earnestly recommend that you prepare and file an honest return, and pay up. The remedy lies not in breaking the law but in amending the law—and the movement toward amendment finally seems to be on the march.

Still, one can do much within the law to lessen the burden of taxes. We shall examine a number of possibilities such as the family partnership, the shuffling of investment income, the use of trusts, the split-estate and so forth. We shall see how a corporation may and may not help its employees keep more of the money they earn. We'll see how one's charitable donations can help in this matter, how to give away money profitably (it can be done!), how to schedule your non-business losses to your tax-advantage, how certain enterprises get a tax-break, and how you may be able simply to move your business out from under the tax burden and at the same time go where people love you.

Some interesting history

Cordell Hull, who drafted the first income tax law in 1913, favored a flat rate of one per cent. However, a graduated scale was adopted which reached the stupendous upper bracket of six per cent upon incomes of more than a half-million (pre-inflation) dollars.

At that time Governor Charles Evans Hughes of New York warned the states against ratifying the Sixteenth Amendment. The Federal tax rate might, he said, "get as high as ten per cent." But Senator Borah replied indignantly to a similar charge by another man:

"Whose equity, sense of fairness, of justice, of patriotism does he question? Why, the representatives of the American people. . . . You can safely rest the power to impose this tax with them."

Time has proven the stern-faced senator from Idaho mistaken. The brackets now rise to a top of 77 per cent—and even our first nibble takes 16 per cent of every dollar in the lowest tax bracket.

What happened, prior to the tax reform? The motion-picture star made one picture a year and quit—he wouldn't work for 9%. Or he set up as an independent producer, for capital gains benefits. The little manufacturer who can't accumulate enough after-tax dollars in his lifetime to pay his estate taxes has to sell out to tax-angle sharpies. Even the bricklayer who used to tend bar in his spare time gave up his second job, because Uncle Sam had moved in as a near-equal partner.

People deliberately earn less; they put ceilings on their ambitions and energies; they refuse to gamble with "safe" dollars by striking out into new business ventures; they will not subsidize with dollars those willing to develop new products; they demolish buildings for tax deductions; they go for tax savings dodges which reduce tax dollars and impair our nation's economy.* They fail to create the new enterprises necessary to employ more persons; in short, capitalism goes on strike and our system of free enterprise comes into jeopardy.

★   *There has been a great deal of our thinking and of our political action molded by a small, insidious group of our population. This, it seems, may be one such measure designed to tear down and to disrupt internal economy, to destroy the "capitalist" incentive. Point 2 in the Communist Manifesto is "A heavy progressive or graduated income tax."*

Yet the swing is to higher and higher taxes—state income taxes piled on top of Federal. The result should be of concern to all of us, because if we destroy the incentive of those who create new employing units, then new employing units cease to appear. And, when this result comes about, then we reap a harvest, as Franklin Delano Roosevelt pointed out, of millions of unemployed and society must pay the toll. We have more opportunity today than ever before in our new technologies, in our demand for new and improved products, and in the need of all people for the benefits of our inventiveness. But we must preserve the rewards for genius and for hard work, as genius unrewarded becomes lazy. If a ven-

* See also the excellent article by Douglas MacArthur, "Taxation; The Hidden Tyrant" in *True*, March, 1958, p. 60.

ture of capital means all risk and no prospect of gain, the funds will remain uninvested.* If new capital is not advanced, there will be no new employing entities and our system of free enterprise is in trouble.

Bearing these things in mind, it is apparent that all of us are deeply concerned about the matter of tax savings and how to retain the maximum benefit of our earnings and investments for the security of ourselves and our families.

If you earn it, you pay

It is difficult to minimize the impact of earned income, in the ordinary situation. Our courts have decreed that the fruit of the tree is attributable to the tree which bears it—and that one whose labor produces the earnings is taxable thereon. He cannot transfer the income, and its consequences, to another, except in limited situations.

One of these would be in the family partnership situation. Here, after bitter years of contest by the Treasury, Congress has intervened in the battle to establish the principle by legislation that a man may create gifts of interests in a partnership. There must be a fair and honest recognition of a return for his efforts, before the other partners will share. Nevertheless, he may, by splitting up such interests among other persons in his family, such as children in low income tax brackets, to whose support he would be contributing in any event, establish a total amount retained out of taxes greater than if he were receiving the entire income. There is an exception, however, to this rule. That is, that the gift must be *bona fide*, and the income must not be used to relieve the taxpayer of his personal obligations. Thus, where

* As stated by the biographer in *Life of an American Workman*, by Walter Chrysler, "But suppose the 1950 scheme of taxation had been in force in that time, especially those provisions of it which limit radically the income any individual may receive. What then? To me, at least, it seems most unlikely that Walter Chrysler would then have exposed his established reputation to great risks of failure. There would have been *no* Chrysler Corporation."

minor children are involved, the wage-earner cannot use such a device to actually receive the money with his left hand and put it in the right hand pants pocket. In such instances, it may necessary to have legal guardians or trustees who are independent of the wage-earner appointed to receive such partnership interests and to represent the minors in that respect.

Likewise, if a family corporation is involved, it is possible to make gifts of stock shares to various members of the family, so as to divide up the dividend income, or to give them specific tasks to do for which they are paid a fair and reasonable consideration.

Another good reason to invest

However, these are palliative remedies, not applicable in the usual situation. Tax savings are of much greater importance in connection with investment earnings. In those situations, the shuffling of interests to multiple taxpayers, each of whose taxes starts at a lower base, or transfers within a family unit to keep such income taxable to one of lower income than the transferor, will result in a lesser payout of total taxes.

Watch that tax bracket

Where investment income is a major source of income, one must consider the fact that this income is received on top of salary income, and therefore at one's top tax rates. If the taxpayer's rate is 48% for salary alone, then all investment income may cost more than half of each dollar received to pay the income taxes thereon. In that case, particularly if one does not need the property for personal security, it is well to divide it up among children who may have little or no personal income. By doing so, perhaps only one-fourth will be payable in income taxes, leaving a full 33⅓% more net investment income available for total family needs than if father had retained ownership. And if the children are minors, and the annual income to each is less than $600, it may escape income taxation entirely.

If the child is at an age too young to supervise such investment, a trust can be created, as heretofore referred to—provided no strings are held back by the donor, that full ownership is actually transferred for the child, and provided further that the income is not used to relieve the father of his duty to support the child. And if the money is used to pay for a college education, it is well to have the institution bill the child directly.

The short-term trust

The use of trusts has led to the development of short-term or Clifford trusts. Let us say that a 45-year old physician, whose earnings place him in the 50% bracket, wants to save for retirement. To reduce shrinkage in income from securities he may create a trust for the benefit of his wife ending, let us say, when the physician reaches age 60. He deposits $50,000 of securities in the trust, paying an average annual return of $3,000. The trustee receives and reports the income at a low rate, with credit for the fiduciary income tax exemption. At the end of the fifteen-year period, the trustee turns over to the wife the accumulated dividends (which, in turn, were re-invested with additional earnings) less income taxes amounting, on the average, to a total remainder of $35,000—or approximately $15,000 more than if Dr. Jones had received those dividends at a greater than 50% income tax rate. He returns the original securities to Dr. Jones, probably enhanced in value by the passage of time. The retirement fund has then grown, given sound management and normal investment cycles, to close to $90,000 or more returning an annual dividend income of, perhaps, $5,000.

In addition to income tax savings, sound planning requires consideration of Federal estate taxes, state inheritance taxes, administration expenses, and shrinkage which might result from forced liquidation of estate assets at figures below their values to pay claims and other charges. For estate tax purposes, all property in which the decedent had an interest at the time of his death is included—even joint tenancy property and life insurance which he has made expressly payable to his wife or children. The first $60,000 of such estate is exempt from Federal taxes, the rate thereafter commencing at 3% and rising to a top of 77%. State inheritance taxes usually increase in proportion to the size of the bequest and the remoteness of kinship of the legatee. All of such items may bite off substantial chunks of a poorly planned estate.

The split-estate

One method of accomplishing savings in estate taxes is by the use of the marital deduction, or split-estate method, in a man's will. He may leave up to one-half of his estate outright to his widow free from estate tax, those assets then being subject to tax in her estate if they remain at that time. The other half he may leave to a trustee in such a way that his widow may receive the income of it, if that is what he wants to accomplish. That half only will be taxed in the man's estate but it will escape taxation in his widow's estate. Various methods of using all or portions of the marital deduction will suggest themselves, depending upon the situation.

Save by giving away

Another method of reducing potential estate taxes is by giving away portions of the estate while one is living. By proper planning, one can give large portions to his children during his lifetime with no tax consequences—and, in any event, a gift tax will usually be far less than the comparable estate tax on the same property or money. There are several reasons for this: (1) Each spouse has a $3,000 annual exemption as to each donee; (2) Each spouse, in addition to these annual exemptions, has a $30,000 gross exemption which may be consumed before any gifts are subject to gift tax; (3) Since both estate taxes and gift taxes are progressive, the making of a gift normally takes such property from the top of the applicable estate tax brackets and moves it down to the lowest gift tax brackets; (4) The gift tax rate is only three fourths of the estate tax rate upon property in the same tax bracket. The warning must be advanced, however, to make haste slowly and only with the most careful of expert guidance.

The business-split

Business can likewise separate its gross income for greater tax savings. This is of particular importance during periods of abnormally high taxes, such as war years, when excess profit taxes permit little profit. When it can be done conveniently, without too much additional bookkeeping and other expenses, and particularly where strong growth is expected, it is well to keep allied but different enterprises segregated. Thus, persons interested in common operations could have one corporation for an automobile dealership, another for a garage, still another for an accessories store. It is important, however, to act only upon mature deliberation after taking all problems into consideration.*

Two-way tax credit

The Treasury is now beginning to crack down upon so-called "fringe benefits." For years, corporations have been favoring top brass by furnishing them with rent-free apartments, club memberships with tabs picked up by the corporation, vacation cruises, automobiles, and other items which would otherwise represent substantial expenditures by those

* For varying suggestions, see the annual *Year End Tax Savings Guide*, published by Research Institute of America, New York.

individuals. However, some of these are legitimate items for a corporation to continue to furnish, where a proper business purpose can be shown. It is of particular importance for every executive to keep close track of expenditures for travel, entertainment, and other expenses related to his employment. For these the employer can reimburse him, with impunity. Meals furnished strictly "for the convenience of the employer" do not represent taxable items. And arrangements can be made for the payment of those fringe benefits which are legitimate in character.

There is a provision now by which $5,000 can be received by an employee's widow, upon his death, free from tax, yet with the employer receiving credit upon the corporate income tax for such payment. While small, that is a desirable item. Deferred income arrangements are desirable. If they are contingent in character and not fixed in amount, they will not be taxed to an individual until payment is actually received. In this way, instead of receiving a terrific income during high tax years and none upon retirement, one can reduce his income during his more productive years and receive a continued income upon retirement, when his income taxes are lower. This is generally paid in return for an agreement not to compete and also to render advice when asked. Stock option arrangements are frequently combined with executive plans. Under these, an officer can be given a three-year option to purchase five thousand shares at the market or slightly above. Then if he helps to make the business boom and doubles the value of the stock, he can sell the option, or buy the stock and sell it—all at capital gains rates —or merely buy the stock and hold it.

Pensions pay

Pension plans, as mentioned above, are not for the executive alone. Under the Prentice-Hall pension plan, as projected, even a person of moderate income could retire, after forty years of service, with an accumulation of three quarters of a million dollars—all upon a capital gains basis. This is due to (a) high return from investment in its own business; (b) tax-free accumulations; (c) lapsing of short-term interests of people who quit the company, their portions swelling the pot.

For a number of years, there has been considerable abuse of oil interests. For example, in one case the taxpayer contracted with a builder to erect for him a substantial house. He conveyed his oil royalty to the contractor to retain and collect all royalties up until a point above the purchase price, then to reconvey it to the taxpayer. The Tax Court upheld the taxpayer's claim that he need pay tax only as portions of his house were erected, to the extent of those proportionate parts over his proportionate bare cost for the property, and upon a capital gains basis. In another situation, a man created a charitable corporation, conveyed his oil royalty to the charity to be returned after it had collected a certain sum in royalties, and took from it a series of notes in a lesser sum to be repaid over a period of years. Again, he successfully claimed a capital gains basis. However, the United States Supreme Court now has apparently seen through some of these devices, and it is unlikely that they will be used as freely in the future.

The charitable foundation

However, there are legitimate methods of tax savings by the use of charitable devices, whereby both the taxpayer and the charity may benefit, and legitimately so. For example, wealthy persons frequently have in mind leaving large amounts to charity, but wait to do so until the times of their deaths. This is most expensive, taxwise. It is far better to form a charitable corporation in one's lifetime, for the purpose of benefiting any charities he desires. So, let us set up the facts of a hypothetical case.

Adam Smith, let us say, owns a family business. When he created it, each of his 10,000 shares of stock was worth

$1 a share. Now each is worth $150 a share. If he should sell, his capital gain would be tremendous—but he doesn't want to sell, in any event, and thus drag strangers into the business. Furthermore, his income puts him in an 80% tax bracket.

So Adam Smith creates the Adam Smith Charities, Inc. Each year he gives the charitable foundation enough stock to use up his 20% charitable exemption. This releases his ready cash, otherwise needed to be used for tax purposes, so as to give him—let us say (since figures must vary from year to year)—$16,000 more personally spendable income each year. By giving to the charity, he may credit his charitable exemption by the amount of $150 per share, but under present case law he need pay no capital gains tax upon the gift. And since the charity need pay no income tax upon dividends, the money from dividends really begins to pile up in its coffers—actually more than three times as fast as in Adam Smith's hands, even with his new exemption.

Adam Smith can then provide for management of the charitable foundation. While ownership of the stock may be divided between him and the charity, if members of the family control both, no stranger will disrupt the family picture. The ready cash in the foundation's treasury permits purchase of much of Adam Smith's remaining stock at his death, to pay debts and estate taxes, and to avoid its being thrown upon the market for forced sale. And since the foundation then has large funds for good deeds, gifts through it to the Community Chest, Salvation Army, or other worthwhile objectives save many personal demands upon members of the family.

Take another example. Jeffrey Ellis is, let us say, 56 years of age. He wants to retire and his tastes are simple— $300 a month income will keep him in comfort, if it is tax free or nearly so. He would like to divide his assets among his children while they are young enough to enjoy them, except for $100,000 which he wants to give to his college scholarship fund. So he sells $100,000 of securities to that fund for an amount of $300 a month for so long as either he or his wife shall live. That fund collects more than the required payment in dividends, pays the monthly annuities, and has a large endowment upon the deaths of the annuitants. And Ellis has an infinitesimal income tax problem, under the present annuity rules.

How to donate an insurance policy

Or, let us say, we are hit for a $10,000 donation for a church foundation. We cannot afford such a payment now. So we decline but say that we will buy a life insurance policy in the amount of $10,000 payable to the foundation. A short-term charitable trust is then created, securities placed in the trust in an amount sufficient to pay the premiums upon a ten-pay life policy, and what is the result? The trust receives the dividends tax free and the policy is paid for painlessly—instead of income taxes coming out of our funds as a result of our personally receiving those dividends. In addition, we receive credit on our income tax for the present value of that ten-year gift, upon our 20% charitable exemption, so that our act of charity may cost us but little in after-tax dollars. Or, if we had not bothered with a trust, if the gift of the policy to the charity had been absolute, our payments of the premiums would constitute annual charitable gifts.

One making a gift to charity is well advised to give property—not money—if that property has appreciated in value. A farmer may give to his church a pig which it may sell, or he may give an undivided one-fourth interest in his growing crops; similarly an investor may give a share of stock which has quadrupled in value. If the owner in each such instance had sold and given money, his money would have been reduced by the tax upon the earning or gain; he receives a charitable exemption for the market value of the gift, if he gives property, but the gift upon income or gain is eliminated. And in some instances he has received a second tax break by the deduction for the cost of producing the item, such as the pig or crop so donated, although the Treasury is not happy over this result.

An older person who is not planning a charitable gift should, however, retain appreciated property as a part of his estate. If he sells it, he will have to pay a capital gains tax. In his estate, however, such property takes on a new value based upon its market at that time, and the estate may then sell it at such valuation without income tax consequences.

Another way to give—and get

One can, under certain circumstances, make money by giving it away—but it takes a high tax bracket to do it. Joe Doakes wants to make a gift of stocks to his children. These securities now bring him in $5,000 a year in dividends. Doakes, the next two years, if he is in a 75% tax bracket, would have only $2,500 left of these dividends. So he creates a trust providing that the Salvation Army shall receive these dividends for the next two years and that the stocks then go to the children. For income tax purposes, he will receive a credit for charitable deduction of approximately $9,200 and a tax savings of $7,150. Doakes then has $4,650 more money than if he had not been so charitably inclined. Of course, such gift must be integrated with his total program; and if his children had little or no income from other sources, the family unit would be dollars ahead if the gift were out-right to the children.

Right at this moment, cattle ranches operating upon a cash basis have a vast advantage over other wage-earners or enterprises. They may raise cattle, create a breeding herd, and all elements of such breeding herd (qualifying under the tests of the Regulations and cases) may be sold upon a capital gains basis, instead of as ordinary income.

When to sell your stock

One selling a security is generally well advised to sell immediately before a dividend, rather than immediately after. Usually the stock decreases in price by the amount of the dividend so declared. Therefore, if held until after dividend, the dividend constitutes ordinary income, while the capital gain is diminished. Prior to dividend, only capital gain is involved, if held for more than six months.

Stocks with large dividend arrears are often good buys, where they have fine prospects. Then, when the financial position moves sharply upward, a sale can be made before the dividends are paid up.

Puts and calls are often used for several purposes. These are the right to sell or to buy a stock at a determined price. One can then keep a loss within the $1,000 tax limit for non-business losses, hedging his investment, yet pay only a comparatively small premium for this security. Of course, they should be used only where a sweeping change in the market, either upward or downward, is expected. One can, by this method, also help to control gains by keeping them in the long-term category, or to establish short-term losses.

At the present time, one can report the interest increment upon E, F, and J government bonds either at maturity or during the holding period. Thus, one may report accrued interest in a year when other income is low, or follow the usual "put off until tomorrow" method, if his income is regularly substantial.

Tax breaks when you guarantee a loan

One should try, wherever possible, to limit non-business losses or to time them properly to offset short-term gains, since one can deduct only up to $1,000 a year, with an additional five-year carry-forward privilege. Speaking of such losses, instead of lending money to a closed corporation, one should have it borrow money from a bank and guarantee the loan. If the corporation fails—then, under the direct loan method, the loss would be of a non-business type limited to $1,000 in any one year, unless his business happened to be that of making loans to such corporations; under the second method, if the guaranteed loan is paid off after the corporation is liquidated, it is fully deductible—and, in some courts, even prior to liquidation. However, this is now subject to challenge, so that one must expect a battle from Uncle Sam.

Real estate "outs"

Cancellation of a lease may be a capital gain to a lessee paid to release his contract. The same may be true of other types of contracts or interests. And some gains or recoveries may be completely non-taxable. For example, if someone smashes my $4,000 automobile and injures me, as well—it would be to my interest to settle my property damage claim for $500 and my personal injury claim for $10,000. The property damage represents a casualty loss to me, if not caused by my fault; the personal injury recovery is received free from tax. Nor does it pay for me to economize by carrying inadequate liability insurance. If one must dig down into his pocket to pay damages to another, caused by his negligence, these losses are not deductible.

There are advantages, frequently, in trading like property for like property, rather than selling one's own property and having to pay a tax upon the gain, and then repurchasing the other property. The little investor may buy a two unit dwelling, improve it, increase his equity in it, then trade it for a larger unit with a larger mortgage—and continue this process until he owns multiple units, without ever having paid a capital gains tax.

Incidentally, where one has substantial dividend income from securities, there is a tax advantage to owning his own home. In that event, the reserve funds may be used for the acquisition of the home, which eliminates or reduces the dividend income. Otherwise, one must receive the dividend income, pay the income taxes upon it, and then use the income which remains after the payment of taxes for the payment of rentals. In addition, there are specific deductions which a home owner may have, in computing income tax credits, such as the interest paid upon the mortgage, real estate taxes paid, and certain casualty losses—as opposed to the income tax which he has been paying upon earnings.

It pays to pay for good advice

It would take a text longer than this work to cover the subject adequately. One should always seek sound advice in preparation of his tax returns, and should seek such advice prior to the end of the year when his CPA or tax attorney will be crowded with a hundred other returns. It is necessary, of course, to keep careful records in order to secure deductible credits upon the income tax returns. It is also necessary to keep careful records of any business transaction. But, when accurate records are kept, and the full problem is laid out to the person preparing the returns, if he is qualified and capable, many little suggestions may be made. For example, where one depreciates an automobile or a truck in his business, it may be profitable for him to purchase new vehicles for cash, rather than trading in the old, and subsequently selling the old vehicles for cash—reporting any gain upon the resale over the depreciated value as capital gain. A man divorced from his spouse should arrange to have alimony, in the usual situation, paid over a period in excess of ten years, rather than in a lump sum, in order to secure tax credit therefor. If he purchases or sells real estate, he should make certain that he receives proper credit for the proportionate part of the property taxes attributable to his interest. And there are many other factors to be considered.

As a final tax savings method, various countries and island possessions are giving special tax consideration, generally for five years, to persons establishing new industries in that area. Thus, one might well establish a business in a preferred portion of the West Indies, operate tax free or nearly so for the period in question, and then liquidate, sell the business, or continue its operation. The heavy tax savings may, in many cases, create a retirement fund. Such an enterprise may be only one facet of a man's holdings or it may occupy his exclusive interest. Each must determine the relative advantage of such features in his general plan.*

These are only a few of the many tax savings and tax investment features available in present-day society. It is unfortunate that, because of a mistaken government tax policy, based upon the doctrine of stripping the diligent of his earnings, and devising elaborate escape hatches, such devices become necessary.

★ *As it is, however, no one should conduct a business enterprise, or undertake personal affairs of importance, without explicit tax guidance of the most expert type. Such assistance will repay its cost many times over.*

PRACTICAL POINTERS

1. You can minimize earned income through the correct use of family partnerships.
2. You can minimize investment income through lifetime gifts to children or the creation of trusts.
3. Estate taxes can be saved through gifts and other plans.
4. Businesses can save by creating several different corporations.
5. Not only does charity open up the heart—it may save money.

* See the discussion in John W. Hughes, "Some Observations on Favorable Tax Investments," *Taxes*, November, 1952, Commerce Clearing House.

13

Don't Rock the Family Financial Boat

ONE'S FAMILY is very important to one's earning power. The man whose personal extravagance, or that of his family, leaves him no resources for expansion may be licked before he starts. At the very least he will be a harassed, tense individual unable to operate at peak efficiency.

It is at the family level, too, that most men get started. And the family, of course, is our basic social group. This chapter deals with a family's finances, and I do not mean a rich family. As I said a while back, it's important to guard the money you have as it is to earn more money. The family level is where guarding your money begins.

We'll look at installment buying, then, and at personal credit. We'll see how a lot of household money can be frittered away, and steps to take to prevent this. We'll go into home ownership versus renting. We'll look at the complicated business of owning a car, and I shall be glad to discuss the steps that protect you when you buy a car on time or buy a used car.

Insurance is very important and we'll give it its due. We'll see some ways to take inexpensive but interesting vocations. Get-rich schemes will take some attention, along with various rackets that take money from people who can't afford it.

Be just a little patient

You can't force the situation which will make you money. If you try to do so, or if you believe the postman never rings twice, you'll go broke. You've got to be alert, but you must also be patient. Study, test, and then act. And when you do act, it should be with deliberation, speed and courage. As I look out my window, near the pond I see a white birch tree sparkling after a spring shower. I remember that two years ago I wondered whether this tree would ever develop. For about three years it had seemed almost dormant, apparently, while its roots were getting settled and seeking strength deeper within the earth. Then suddenly last year it shot up to double its former size, the bark turned white, and it is now a mature tree, serene in its beauty.

You can't begin at the top

Most married couples want to begin life with the things their parents ended their careers with, after a lifetime of saving—a home, a car, a houseful of furniture, children, possibly a country club, and no bills. Even Plato never attained such a state in his Republic. It takes time, and patience, to achieve these ultimate objectives. Like the white birch, after their roots have settled deeply, they may suddenly find that, over those years, they have achieved financial security. But, if this need for time, for patience, and for intelligently directed activity is not realized, young people are going to be battered in their egos, and another bankrupt couple may face a shattered marriage. Children of the depression, such as are those of us of middle years, are perhaps overconscious of financial needs and possible insecurities. This is, perhaps, in its way as bad as the attitudes of those who have been born within the last twenty-five years, who have personally never experienced any depressions or any economy other than one sustained on a war level or by government spending.

Perhaps the quickest way to attain financial security is to inherit money or to marry a rich woman—or for a woman to marry a rich man. That has its disadvantages, as well as its advantages. However, for the remaining ninety-nine per cent of us, it is necessary to accumulate those funds which we need either for primary security or as investment capital from our own earnings. This means, unfortunately, that habits of thrift must be developed, as the amount of one's earnings is immaterial if every cent of income is spent. If all is spent to try to match our parents' slowly earned luxuries, we can accumulate no such reserve. As stated by that eminent philosopher, Micawber, in *David Copperfield*:

> "Annual income twenty pounds, annual expenditure nineteen six, result happiness. Annual income twenty pounds, annual expenditure twenty pounds ought and six, result misery."

Translated into dollars, the meaning is equally clear—and equally accurate.

Trouble starts "on time"

Two centuries ago, Benjamin Franklin said:

> "Buy what thou hast no need of and e'er long thou shalt sell thy necessaries."

Nor was he far wrong. Many persons complain they cannot make ends meet. But too often this is merely an excuse for bad family management.

One of the reasons for family financial disaster is the inability to cope with installment purchases. Many families start in to buy a house on the installment plan, then an automobile, then a living room set, a bedroom set, kitchen appliances, a television set, a washing machine, insurance, and even clothing. Each adds a new weekly or monthly payment on top of other payments—then, if illness occurs, a layoff, or other financial crisis, the family is in real trouble.

Whenever it seems desirable to purchase anything, one should get out his pencil and add up the total of all the payments which will have to be made. He may find an alarming differential between the cash price as advertised and the total of the payments which he will be required to make to own the article in question. Furthermore, he had better carefully examine the proposed conditional sales contract. It may provide that if he falls even one payment behind, the store may retake the article so sold, sell it at private sale at its own discretion, and still hold him responsible for the balance. So he may wind up minus all payments to that time, minus furniture or other article, and with still a substantial obligation upon his hands.

Certainly some investigation should be made of the dealer with whom such responsibilities are to be placed. The Better Business Bureau may be able to furnish information, as may other merchants of established reputation. It should be determined whether the markup for a credit plan is reasonable, whether the dealer sells good or shoddy merchandise, whether he stands in back of the items which he sells, and whether he is quick to repossess or to make trouble with the purchaser's employer. Also, if he is the type who says that the matter is in the hands of the finance company and he can do nothing about it, the customer is in for trouble, because certainly the finance company is not interested in the quarrels of the dealer and the customer.

The hook sinks deep

Frequently, there is no limit to the amount of charge which the merchant can add for "carrying charges." Carrying and finance charges may raise the total to double the original price. This should be realized before one goes deeply in debt. Furthermore, one should beware of the salesman who railroads him into a small-loan office to incur a substantial debt for the purpose of making any purchase. Small loan obligations are not easy to repay. Once the first loan is made, the average borrower is usually good for about seven years as a customer.

Since many people are chronically incapable of avoiding excessive spending so long as they have a checking account, it is often desirable to use a savings account instead. There is something more painful about withdrawing the money and paying out in cash for any purchase. The color of money has a peculiar psychological effect. I remember one time when I was with an old-time claims adjuster, in the upper Michigan peninsula, there was a case that was hard to settle. The people demanded a minimum of $3,000 in settlement. After we had been talking to these people a half hour, the adjuster laid $250 in ten-dollar bills upon the table in front of them. Their eyes began to glisten, but they still shook their heads. After more conversation, he finally added another $250 in ten-dollar bills, and it made an interesting heap upon the table. When they finally still said "No," he started to gather the bills together into a compact bundle, then finally turned to me and asked if I would lend him an additional hundred dollars to close the deal. As they watched the money almost reaching his pocket, they agreed that if I would do that the case would be settled. It was settled, at a substantial saving, because dollars on the table meant more than a settlement figure named at random.

Of course, I like to use checking accounts myself, because a cancelled check constitutes an excellent receipt. It depends upon the temperament of the person. If the person is capable of sound and wise budgeting, then a checking account is desirable. Otherwise, if one must guard against his own impulsiveness, a savings account is much to be preferred.

Establishing credit

Some persons are similarly incapable of using a charge account wisely. In those instances, the existence of a charge account is an invitation to unwise spending. In the case of more rational persons, it is far better to purchase items, charge the cost, and pay the obligation off promptly in order to establish sound credit. A credit rating is never established through paying cash for items, because no credit experience is involved. Similarly, if one makes a small loan at a bank, repays it promptly, and the next time borrows slightly more and repays that, his rating with that bank is bound to be excellent. Such methods are eminently desirable in establishing credit in the first instance.

Where a charge account is available, and it is used wisely, it is far better to charge the cost of necessaries rather than to borrow money at interest to pay the cost. However, one should look out for such things as "revolving charge accounts." This is a device to keep the customer perpetually indebted to the place of business, by tempting him to spend up to the amount of the available credit. That is foolish. In addition, the interest charge frequently amounts to one-and-a-half per cent per month, which is eighteen per cent a year, on the current balance. Many merchants, unfortunately, are willing to sell to persons who cannot really afford to buy, figuring that they can collect through high pressure methods, and are not generally interested in the welfare of the customers. Normally, the better established merchants are more interested in a sound clientele and good customer relationships.

When to borrow

There are times when small loans may be very desirable. Suppose, for example, one must buy furniture. Four years ago some friends of mine had to buy a great deal of furniture. Just at that time, an army captain was being transferred east, and wanted to sell precisely the items they needed. The cost was less than half of what it would have run through a furniture store. Here, the making of a small loan permitted them to make a substantial saving in cost, and yet discharge the obligation in installments.

Usually it is not worthwhile to make a small loan for the purpose of discharging a debt to a hospital or a physician. Normally these persons are accustomed to working with people under financial stress, and will accept installment payments where a regular schedule is set up and religiously followed. They would prefer that these people not incur large interest obligations, in addition to the principal owed. In other words, one should not be panicked into making a small loan, nor persuaded that it is better to have one super-colossal back-breaking loan rather than a multitude of smaller ones. Small loan companies serve an excellent need, properly used and not abused. The conscientious loan manager will be glad to assist those in need in working out their own problems, and prefers not to see any person enmeshed hopelessly in debt.

Many banks have now started small loan departments where they will sit down and help work out the problems of the individual, and at a far greater saving in interest charges. Credit unions are associations usually made up of employees or union members. Members invest money by buying shares, and may borrow money as they need it. Often those resources are available, at reasonable interest, to serve the needs of the members. And, if none is presently available, the members can well organize one.

Guard your insurance

Money may also be borrowed upon a life insurance policy at a reasonable rate of interest. However, since there is no pressure placed by the insurance company for repayment of the loan, a person may forget to make repayment and thereby lose the benefit of the life insurance. It is often better to use such a policy as collateral for a bank loan, where there will be a reminder for repayment. Several years ago, I took some of my life insurance policies and borrowed money at three-and-one-half per cent to pay off a five per cent mortage loan, and then repaid the lower interest-bearing bank loan as funds permitted.

For home improvements, government insured FHA loans are usually easy to arrange. The difficulty is that this has often been used as a sales mechanism for getting people to buy things which they did not need. People are often saddled with many such loans which were absurd, and many of these have been tools for fraud. A few years ago, a man I knew in the loan business had persons sign such applications together with other documents authorizing and directing the payments to be made to the agent. When the checks were received, they were deposited in his account, and the borrowers were ignorant of that fact until they started receiving notices as to payments falling due. One must be extremely careful as to any document calling for the payment of money which he signs; and, if it involves a substantial amount of money, it is worth the payment of a ten-dollar bill to an attorney to glance at it and see if it is in proper shape for signature.

The inescapable expense

One must give thought to all aspects of family finances if they are to be soundly based. Let us take the little matter of food, for example. My mother was a most delightful, and thoroughly impractical, woman. At a time when my father was an army officer with six children, buying enough meat and groceries to feed a football team, instead of comparing prices of meats and groceries, she would run charge accounts at the little neighborhood stores. Following my father's death, one winter, when I was shoveling snow to try to get money together for groceries, etc., we boys had occasion to compare the prices of groceries in those stores and chain stores. There is a great difference now, of course, in such comparative prices, because of the combined purchasing power of the independent grocery associations, etc., but at that time whipping cream was selling for forty cents a half pint in the store where my mother traded, and twenty cents just down the street. Other prices were in proportion. Needless to say, the charge accounts were canceled, and we took over the grocery buying from that point on.

A careful housewife can save countless dollars for her household. It is a question of knowing what to buy, as well as where to buy—the nutritious, but economical, cuts of meat, the times of the year to buy them, the stocking up at times of depressed prices, the proper utilization of meats and vegetables, the making of foods from "scratch," instead of from more expensive prepared or semi-prepared foods, and the like. And, in this regard, seldom is there a worthwhile saving for the small family in the purchase and maintenance of a home freezer. For a farm family, or the very large family, it may be a different story.

Normally it costs more to order upon the telephone and have things delivered. It costs more to buy porterhouse steak than it does to buy round steak. Common sense will indicate many ways to accomplish substantial savings.

Fine feathers

With reference to buying clothes, frequently the men who buy silk suits and the women who wear mink coats are the ones who cannot afford them. The people who have money often don't give a hoot about impressing others, and don't feel the need for an ostentatious wardrobe. Good clothes are not necessarily expensive clothes. So far as suits, shirts, shoes, dresses, and other article of apparel are concerned, as has been demonstrated repeatedly by *Consumer's Guide* and other publications of that type, there are substantial savings which can be made without sacrificing quality.

Even more than the price paid per item, however, is the fact that there often is a lack of planning in the purchase of clothing. One should plan as to what the needs are, cutting those demands to a few simple essentials, and then buy the clothing required to fill those needs. People are liked for themselves, not for what they wear—and the mere fact that a woman buys her dresses on sale does not mean that she has saved any money, if she did not need the dresses she bought.

Let a home wait

It seems to be the fashion for every young married couple now immediately to plan the purchase of a home. There are a number of reasons why I oppose home ownership for very young couples. In the first place, the net savings of principal which are made over this period of time are quite small, if any. It tends to tie them to a specific community and area when often, for purposes of promotion, advancement, and changing jobs, it would be better if they were footloose. It tends to require them to center their interests in a certain locality, rather than in another to which their natural inclinations and friendships, had they waited longer, would have taken them. And it tends to saddle them with a principal responsibility which often later proves to be disadvantageous.

It is not surprising that our young people become trapped into home ownership. The growing ads "no payment down," "two-hundred dollars down," etc., together with low monthly payment schedules, make them feel that it is cheaper to own a home than to rent. They come to regard home ownership as an inalienable right, rather than something to be worked toward. They feel that it increases their maturity and stature to be regarded as home owners, rather than as tenants.

Comes the dawn

If the young prospective home owners are not careful because of their lack of experience, they are liable to find themselves saddled with a house which is too small for their needs, poorly designed, or poorly constructed. It may be in a location which will quickly become obsolete or slummish. It takes some few years of experience to know something about where to build a home, the type of home to build, and something of sound construction, so that a little maturity is a desirable thing. Furthermore, unless they are careful, they are going to find heavy obligations about which the advertisements do not tell them—such as loan application charges, surveys, service charges, and other obligations which can mount rapidly.

In addition to the mortgage payments, the owner must realize that the bulk of the monthly payments will be represented by interest, so that the total of these payments do not represent actual dollar savings. But, in addition to those monthly payments, there are other obligations which must be met at regular intervals, and which add to the expense of home ownership. Some of them are as follows: taxes, fire insurance, liability insurance, special assessments, fuel, utilities, repairs, yard maintenance, and decorating. Nor are these necessarily small items. One should talk to seasoned home owners in the same general price bracket of house and learn from them what their expenses have been over a period of time for each and all of these items, and then prorate over the period of a year to determine what they will be. Experts have stated that one should never pay more than two and a half times his annual income for a house, and that under no circumstances should one's entire capital be tied up in home ownership.

When you are ready to buy a home

Before one enters into any contract for the purchase of a house or the building of a house, he should, of course, have the advice of a good attorney. The title should be checked, and all contract papers should be approved before one's signature appears thereon. Then, assuming everything is in order, and home ownership is definitely desirable in that particular situation, there are a few rules which may be helpful, although they rarely can be completely followed.

1. Buy in an area where automobile traffic is not, and will not become, heavy so as to be dangerous to children.

2. Buy in an area where there are adequate parks or recreational facilities for children.

3. Buy in an area where schools and churches are reasonably close, so that children can easily walk to them, instead of having to be driven thereto, and where they do not have to cross any heavily-trafficked street in reaching them. Conversely, do not buy across the street from a school, church or funeral parlor. These tend to depreciate home values.

4. Buy in an area which has people generally of the same income bracket and of approximately the same age, so that the children will have playmates and so that the neighbors will be persons with similar problems and similar tastes.

5. Be sure that the public transportation facilities are reasonably adequate.

6. If a location is selected because of the lovely trees, be sure that they are of a type that is reasonably disease-resistant.

7. Check through people who know to be sure that the drainage facilities and that the sewage disposal facilities are not only adequate, so that difficulties do not arise in times of heavy rains, but to be sure that they remain adequate if there is a great deal of expanded development in that same area.

8. If you buy a house already built, have it checked thor-

oughly by a competent contractor, and pay him for his services, to be sure that it is solidly and firmly built, has no termites, and that there will be no serious repair problems in the next few years.

9. Be sure to get the largest possible mortgage, with the minimum possible down payment, to make resale possibilities easier in the event you have to sell within a year or two. Be sure that you can pay off any or all of the mortgage with the least possible penalty. Get a mortgage with the lowest possible interest rate, running for the longest possible period of time.

10. Know at all times what you are signing, but always have it checked by a good attorney.

So far as rentals are concerned, one knows where he stands each month, and what proportion of the paycheck will be taken for rental expense. Normally, the rental should not exceed twenty-five to thirty per cent of his income, but this varies widely depending upon circumstances.

This does not mean that I discourage home ownership for people whose roots are thoroughly settled in any community. But I do discourage it until one knows exactly where he is going, where he wants to live, that his tenure in that community will be reasonably permanent, and that the house to be purchased satisfies not only the immediate needs but the reasonably foreseeable needs of the future.

The complicated business of owning a car

A few years ago, Joe Holmes stopped into my office very much disturbed. He was being sued for $600. "How can they sue me?" he demanded to know. "They took away my car just because I missed one payment. They got the car I traded in, and I am walking. How come I still owe them money?"

That seemed a little raw to me, too, so I checked. The conditional sales contract permitted them to repossess and sell at private sale. They sold the new car to an employee at a song. Their service charges, even though the car Joe had bought was a used one, amounted to about $200. We finally worked it out, but I learned then that the finance company works with the bank's money, discounting the paper which it takes in so that it actually has almost no money of its own in circulation at any time, but it reaps its harvest through these substantial service charges, plus the commissions made on insurance when they handle that aspect of it.

For the person who has to buy on a deferred payment plan, of course, it probably is his only method of purchase, and there is no question but that finance companies have frequently gotten the worst end of it from automobile purchasers. Their business is not all gravy. But, for the person possessing the proper kind of credit, it may be better if he finances his purchase through a bank. A number of insurance companies advertise that they will assist their insureds in making bank loans, and normally a bank will be willing to work directly with such a customer.

In buying a car, it is well to know something about the reputation of the dealer, as well as the reputation of the automobile. I referred a person to another attorney to handle his suit against a dealer, which involved a new and not inexpensive car. Apparently, from what I was told, it was a real lemon. Yet the dealer would do nothing to make it good, stating in effect: "Sue me." That type of person generally establishes a reputation pretty quickly among other dealers and persons who know automobiles, and the prospective purchaser would do well to make some inquiries as to how completely the dealer stands in back of his product.

The automobile manufacturers, because of demands of competition, are now extending considerably better warranties than they did a few years ago.

Are you sure you need a car?

Normally, a new automobile can be bought at considerably below the list price, and it is well to get competitive figures concerning vehicles in the same price range. It is also well to be sure one really needs an automobile and can afford the luxury of one before purchasing it. I have always felt that metropolitan dwellers are foolish to buy automobiles, unless absolutely necessary for business reasons. One can afford to ride many taxicabs before paying the cost of depreciation alone upon a car.

Let us say that a new car costs $2,800, and that the average family trades one in every three years. Let us say that the trade-in value at that time is $1,050. That means an average depreciation of $583 a year or almost $50 a month. Insurance will add another $10 a month, gasoline, oil, and repairs at least a dollar a day, and probably closer to $40 a month. This would make in excess of $100 a month, based upon the smaller types of automobiles. The Cadillac owner can double these figures. However you figure it, an automobile is and remains a luxury.

How to buy a used car

If one buys a used automobile, he would be well advised to single out those vehicles which look particularly interesting to him, first trying to obtain the true history of the particular vehicle and the actual mileage, then to employ a competent mechanic and have him go thoroughly over the vehicle. If the mechanic advises against the purchase, it should be forgotten. I know nothing whatever about the innards of an automobile and must necessarily rely upon its history and upon the integrity of the dealer. There are some questions, however, which can well suggest themselves whenever one does look at a used automobile.

1. What is the actual history? From whom was it pur-

chased? Then I would call that person and talk to him about the automobile and his experiences with it. He no longer owns it, and will probably be fairly honest about it.

2. I would rub my hands over the fenders and feel whether they are smooth or rough, as if they had been bumped out. If the paint on any fender looks brighter or newer than any other, I would know that that had been replaced more recently, which also would indicate, as would slight unevenness, that the vehicle had been in a wreck.

3. I would look inside the door for service stickers. Those would tend to indicate the true mileage. If they have been removed, I would want to know the reason why, because they ordinarily would not be.

4. I would want to see the condition of the original upholstery and of the appearance of the car itself. People who keep a car clean and looking good normally are careful of the automobile in other respects.

5. I would look at the tires. If they have the original tires on them, usually the serial numbers of the tires are relatively close, and they will all be of the same make. If they are not, it is an indication that new tires have been added and that the vehicle has been driven at least 20,000 miles, irrespective of what is shown upon the speedometer.

6. If there is a new battery in the automobile, it normally indicates that the automobile has been driven more than 20,000 miles. Similarly, if the brake pedal pad is badly worn, this would be an indication of the same thing.

7. I would want to drive the car and, upon a straight road where no traffic is approaching, release the wheel and see if it tends to float to one side or the other. I would want to accelerate it suddenly at different speeds, and to see if there is any shimmy or pull. And I would want to listen to the sound of the motor, although I know enough about automobiles to know that motor noises can often be concealed for short periods of time.

8. I would want to check the doors, slam them, close them gently, and also study the fitting of them to see if there

is any misalignment. If there is, it is often another indication that a car has been wrecked. Similarly, if the trunk lid does not fit securely or leaves an air gap, the same may be indicated.

9. If, when the engine is cold, the car is permitted to idle and one accelerates a few times, and blue smoke pours from the exhaust, this is an indication that the engine is burning oil.

The best method is, still, to buy from a dealer of integrity, but the mere fact that he has a big place of business, or is successful financially, does not necessarily mean that. We are rather fortunate, in small communities such as I live in, in knowing the businessmen rather intimately and being able to do business in reliance upon their characters. It is more difficult, frequently, in larger communities to do as well, but there are still dealers of the same high integrity in all areas, if one only becomes acquainted with them.

Furnishing your nest

The same rules of sound purchasing, and not buying what one does not need, applies to the acquisition of furniture. It is not necessary to buy five rooms of furniture all at one time.

The first apartment that Jean and I lived in was a one-and-one-half room efficiency apartment. We had a teetery spinet desk which she had used as a child; we bought an old metal army cot, padded it, and covered it with 10-cents-a-yard material, and this became our couch; we had an old dinette set with four wooden chairs which we painted ourselves, and a nine-by-twelve Axminster rug which we bought on sale for $29.75. I forgot to mention an old rocking chair which had belonged to her aunt. That was our initial furniture, and it served us well until we could replace it.

★   *One does not have to excel the Joneses. Your friends enjoy you; they do not come to look at your furniture, nor to appraise your assets. Build-*

*ing up from nothing can be fun, if only people
would stop to realize it.*

Insurance guards you

But there is more to the art of budgeting than the acquisition of physical things. Every budget should provide for
paying insurance premiums. The insurance, in turn, provides
the money you need, if you need it, to protect against ruin-
ing your entire personal economy with some catastrophic
loss.

Most people know how an automobile accident can ruin
an uninsured person, or one who has insufficient insurance.
Unfortunately there are so many accidents that this factor is
well publicized. Yet many persons are still grossly under-
insured. I know one family that had to mortgage their home
to the hilt to pay off the consequences of a moment's in-
attention on the road—and this was in addition to payment
from their insurance, which was paid to its limit.

Also you should have a comprehensive personal liability
policy, which covers you against damage you may do when
you slice a golf ball, or leave a child's roller skate where someone will step on it. If you own property other than your
home, you may want what is commonly called an OL&T
policy, or owner's, landlord's and tenant's liability insurance.
If other people work for you, it is desirable to carry workmen's compensation insurance. Then of course you'll want
fire insurance on the full value of your home, and definitely
you'll want medical insurance to meet the costly emergencies
of sickness, accident, or prolonged therapy of any kind. I'll
discuss life insurance separately.

The best way to arrange an adequate program of insurance
is to find a good, reputable broker and have him handle all
the policies, except life insurance, through good companies.
Having a single broker will save you from listening to a
dozen competing agents on each coverage. Your broker will
help arrange renewal dates to fall at times that do not conflict

with other financial burdens. Be sure to check the advantages of paying by the year, if possible, rather than at shorter intervals, since you can almost always save money. Some insurance is best arranged on a three- or five-year basis, payable annually.

Your life insurance

Life insurance should be the first major purchase by a family unit, even before the purchase of a home. It is the only means by which a young couple can buy a ready-made estate on the installment plan to protect the wife and children in the event of the premature death of the wage-earner. This is no time, in those early years, for frills—such as educational policies for the children, retirement income insurance, or high cost insurance. A young friend of mine called me a few months ago, after his first child was born, to ask what I thought about the advisability of purchasing an insurance policy to cover the education of his first-born child. I told him it was nonsense; they were having a difficult time even paying the rent at that time. Eighteen years from then, he could probably well afford to send that child through college; or, if he could not, she could work part time. Furthermore, the dollars which were so hard to come by now, if inflation continued, might be worth only half as much when such a policy matured. I told him to concentrate now on getting sufficient insurance to take care of his daughter in the event he should die, not insurance to send her through college in the event he should then be alive.

What the young couple should buy is a substantial amount of convertible term insurance with a sound major company with whom they would be willing to carry their insurance program the rest of their lives; and, if it is a participating contract (that is, one paying dividends), let the dividends reduce the insurance cost. As they can afford it, they should convert units of the term insurance into ordinary life insurance—and, if their means are then ample, the dividends can be permitted to accrue to pay up the insurance more quickly. In that manner, the family members have received immediate protection, they have guarded against the risk of later uninsurability of the wage-earner, and, as means have permitted, they have embarked upon a retirement program. And, by all means, waiver of premium provisions in the event of disability should always be included in such contracts. Some of the newer forms of contracts permit insurance against the hazard of becoming uninsurable—a most important protection at minimal cost.

Mutual stock and companies

The majority of life insurance is issued by mutual companies. Those contracts are termed "participating" policies, which term means, simply, that a portion of the premium is returned annually in the form of dividends. Such dividends can be used either to reduce the premium, to shorten the premium paying period, or to add to the policy protection.

Policies issued by stock companies are usually "non-participating,," although they could be issued in a participating form, which means that they are figured upon a net cost basis and return no dividends. The gross premiums quoted upon such insurance are always lower, but the question of ultimate net cost depends upon the particular company and its experience over a period of years.

The premium which the insured pays is divided into two parts: (1) net premium—which is, in turn, subdivided into (a) current year mortality element; (b) current year increased policy reserves—and (2) expense loading. It is obvious that the mortality element, or risk of death, increases each year. That is one reason why insurance costs less when taken at an earlier age. Not only is the mortality risk less, but the company has the use of the money longer with which to secure earnings and thus to increase the policy reserve. These earnings from the policy reserve are carefully computed with the mortality element in order to establish a "level premium," which is not subject to increase as the insured grows older.

How your need changes

The cost of the mortality feature would be the same at the age 35 irrespective of the kind of insurance which the insured carries. The larger the premium paid, the more there is left to accumulate at interest to pay off the policy more quickly, or to add to the savings feature. During the early years, when earnings are less, one is foolish to put any more into the savings feature than is required; later, when other savings and assets are sufficient to guard against the loss arising from the wage-earner's death, one is interested in boosting the savings feature as much as possible. For the young man, in simple terms, the goal should be large protection and small savings features; for the older man, thinking of retirement, large savings features and less insurance protection.

Life insurance has great values to the family. Its settlement options, for example, provide flexible means of payments to a widow or children without the expense of a trustee, and make sure that rent, utilities, food, and medical expenses may be paid after the wage-earner has passed on. Life insurance has limitations as well. If the person is in an earning bracket where he can accumulate equity savings as well as dollar savings, his entire resources should not be in a life insurance program. And, so far as fixed-dollar annuities are concerned, I would seldom recommend them except in a situation where a person is mentally or psychologically incapable of administering his own funds—such as many motion picture stars or other performers. Even in that event, usually I would prefer management by a corporate trustee.

Some money in the bank

In the preceding discussion, we have discussed, in the main, the primary sources of family expenditure, operating as a unit. We have discussed the acquisition of a home versus rental accommodations, a car, furniture, food, clothing, insurance, and other expenditures. It is apparent that all of these must be synchronized into a sound, well-working arrangement which will meet the needs of that particular group within the safe limits of the funds available. And, from those resources, a savings program should be created. There should always be some emergency funds which are available if disaster strikes, or if great opportunity arises. Then the income should be budgeted to cover the various family needs.

And yet, in all the planning for saving, it should be borne in mind that every individual, and every family, must live each day at a time, and not destroy the pleasures of living by frugality or stinginess to a point where life becomes meaningless.

★   *The last is not likely to happen. The true pleasures in life are normally not bought; they are lived. The taste of a single bite of chocolate, savored in its excellence, can be as satisfying as devouring a pound of candy, and be much better for the figure, as well. The kindness of people, the pleasures of conversation, the enjoyment of music, the beauties of nature, are largely free.*

Getting tough with yourself

In situations where people have trouble budgeting, or in refraining from spending more than their income, they must take more drastic steps. In such situations, some folks make up separate envelopes for each item in the budget, and put the salary when received into that many envelopes and put it aside immediately. If they need written receipts for their money, they can pay by money orders, where the maintenance of a checking account gives them too much temptation. But sometimes a family unit will find itself in deep water from which it appears that it can never emerge. In that event, its members must (1) make a list of every obligation which is owing; (2) set down the amount of salary available to meet present and past obligations; (3) set down the present scale of spending, and the method in which it is divided; (4) determine precisely how present spending can be cut; (5) determine how much that will leave out of salary to meet past obligations; (6) work out a practical method of discharging past obligations which will permit some payment to be made upon each account every month; (7) draw up the plan in writing and present it to each of the past creditors, and secure an agreement from them to go along with the plan; (8) keep the obligation to the letter. If any emergency should arise, such as unexpected illness which will delay fulfillment, notify each creditor immediately.*

Normally, any reasonable businessman will go along with a plan of this type. If he refuses to, it is well to explain the whole situation to the other creditors, and they may well bring pressure upon the recalcitrant one to force him to go along. Otherwise, it may be explained to the local Credit Bureau and they may assist in getting his acceptance. If he then still refuses, and the obligations are tremendous in size, the matter can be presented to a competent attorney who can help the family to work out its problems.

New lands, new people

Family vacations are an important matter. They are great refreshers of the body and the spirit and they are well worth saving for. But there are ways to save on the actual vacation itself, especially on traveling.

There is a vast difference, for example, in transportation costs "during the season" and "off season." † If the saving of

---

* As to the importance of a sound plan in time of crisis, see Sidney Margolius' article "How to Face a Financial Crisis" in *Coronet*, September, 1958, p. 52.

† For example, see Tom Mahoney's article "Travel Without Tears," *Reader's Digest*, August, 1958, p. 186; K. C. Jerome, "How to Save While Spending," *Family Weekly*, June 8, 1958.

time is not important, many find it completely delightful to travel by freighter.* Special family rates can be secured upon certain days of the week upon airlines and many railroads. One can secure special tours through the Canadian railroads, or upon British railroads by purchasing in advance their thrift coupons, and the Danish railroads give reduced rates to the elderly upon week-days. A favorable rate of dollar exchange made it cheaper to fly to South America in 1958 than in 1957. Of course, one should always carry his excess funds in traveller's checks—not cash.

There are great variations in hotel and food costs in different parts of the world and these fluctuate with some rapidity.† Many picturesque, delightful islands of the Atlantic, parts of Spain, and other colorful portions of the world are bargains compared to U.S.A. prices—and leisurely travel need not be expensive. Any good librarian can help those interested to find articles concerning those place where the pension dollars will go far, while permitting glimpses into these romantic spots.

Look out for "come-ons"

Beware of advertisements which promise fabulous money-making opportunities. Some of these are legitimate; many are not. Most of those which seem to offer opportunities at very low cost usually offer only advice and not income.

One of the favorite advertisements is to "make money sewing." The implication is that the person advertising will purchase everything sewed by the individual. Actually, all they are doing is selling material to the individual, who still has to find his own buyers. The same is generally true of the advertisements to "make money addressing envelopes." Usually the instructions received for the payment do nothing

* J. C. Furnas, "Have You Got That Freighter Bug?", *Saturday Evening Post*, July 5, 1958, p. 22.

† See, for example, the Harian Publications, Greenlawn, New York.

more than give some hints as to how to solicit typing business. The advertiser has no market for the individual desiring the income.

Others offer to sell equipment which will enable one to make from $75 to $200 a week, as the usual form of the offer reads. These run all the way from popcorn, to the manufacture of potato chips, to metal-plating babies' shoes. In such circumstances, not only must one part with a substantial initial amount of money, but he is usually embarking into a field about which he knows nothing and in which he must create the market. It is not quite so simple as it sounds from the advertisement, and one would be well advised to check with persons in a like business, in other communities, before making such investment. Newspaper and magazine advertisements must be scrutinized with a great deal of caution.

Other advertisements are cleverly worded to separate one from his money without setting him up in business. These include such things as patent medicines, reducing pills, insulin substitutes, vitamin pills, love potions, and devices to make a woman more bosomy. However, it is normally better to secure medical information from his own physician and pharmaceuticals from his own drugstore. It is also better to deal with known reputable landscape houses.

The "cons" of con-games

There have been fantastic schemes whereby thousands of people have each subscribed hundreds of dollars over a period of years in order to share in completely fictitious estates, such as the fabulous Drake Swindle.* Or, these people are notified that they themselves have inherited sums of money but that they must send $100 or $1,000 to Mr. X for preliminary expenses thereon. In the case of orthodox estates, these can always be verified through a local attorney who

* This is described fully in the *Family Weekly*, June 29, 1958, p. 12.

can soon ascertain whether the matter is legitimate or not. And other minor rackets include such things as notifying a person that he has won a homesite or some acreage in some remote state, but that he needs to send $100 for the purpose of checking the title and recording fees, etc. It may turn out that he has a square foot of land under water in some Florida bay.

Other common fraudulent schemes to watch out for are such gimmicks as inducing a customer to sign a purchase contract in blank, whereupon higher sales figures are filled in; conducting a contest where everyone wins a prize—such as ten dollars off on an expensive piece of merchandise; gyp home study courses; positions for "supervisors" or "route managers"; and other advertisements where almost anyone can obviously qualify.* And, incidentally, just as a free tax tip from a lawyer, you can seldom afford to win prizes on a quiz show. If you keep them, you are taxed on the alleged retail value—and most of them are junk you can't use. A woman on the Groucho Marx program one evening revealed that she had won $26,000 in prizes upon a different program—including a $3,000 gold-plated lawnmower and similar items. Warned of the tax dangers, she and her husband disposed of them all, after a year of struggle, for a total of $1,200. Their taxes would have been at least four times that amount.

Another racket which is being worked at the moment is one where the swindler studies the obituary columns and reads the recent notices of death. He then addresses a letter to the deceased person, which arrives a few days after his death, telling him that he is now in need of funds himself and he would appreciate it if the deceased would return the hundred dollars he borrowed on such and such a date. He makes enough of a survey regarding the deceased so as to supply plausible details. Or he may send merchandise which was supposedly ordered, or deliver something to the house on

* Don Wharton, "Five Swindles to Watch Out For," *Reader's Digest*, August, 1958, p. 72.

which a certain balance is due, perhaps some luxury which the deceased supposedly had ordered for his wife as his last act. In almost all instances, the distraught widow pays over the money requested. This is a heartless and loathsome swindle, and, where the widow has any reason to be suspicious, she should certainly notify the police and let them at least investigate the matter.

In time of death

The occasion of death, almost inevitably, leads to considerable expense. A dignified funeral and a simple stone can be had for five or six hundred dollars; but I have seen families, almost destitute, contract for a service costing fifteen hundred dollars and a monument that cost five hundred dollars on top of that.

Such people will tell you, and believe, that they bankrupt themselves out of respect for the dead. But they really act out of vanity, the same old human vanity you'll meet everywhere. They merely are keeping up with their relations who show equal vanity in the adjoining cemetery plot.

My final advice to a family that wants to guard its resources: Money was not meant to be buried. It's a big help in life, and when you go you can't take it with you. Remember that.

PRACTICAL POINTERS

1. Don't get so involved in installment purchases that you may fall behind in time of crisis. And remember, you pay for the installment privilege.
2. Use loans only in time of real need, unless a genuine saving can be accomplished by the loan.
3. Don't buy a home till you know you are ready to settle and stay in one place.
4. Plan a wise insurance program. Your life insurance

—just one part of the program—gives you values that nothing else can give.

5. Beware of any proposition that looks too good.
6. Find out the ways to buy wisely, the ways to live modestly and the ways to budget for what you really want.

★   *Neither I nor anyone else can tell you everything that helps you increase your money-making capacity and guard the money you make. I have tried to select significant things, bearing in mind I am writing only one book of convenient size.*

But if you have followed through with me, I believe you now own at least a good basic knowledge of what makes the money-wheels go 'round. You know where to look for money-making possibilities, how to gauge your own capacity to handle them, and how to handle them if they really are for you.

You have gained, I hope, the conception that money is something more than a crinkle in your billfold. You know how money makes credit, and how relatively small amounts of money can swing great weight at the right time. You know the major hows and whys of stocks and other securities. Above all, you know the enormous power of money to make money.

By sharing the experiences of some very successful men, I hope you have come to see the basic requirements of success, and why it goes hand in hand with hard work and enthusiasm. Also you have seen where failure comes from; how the seeds of disaster can be sown—and watered and fertilized, too—with the same energy that brings success when it is well-directed.

We've sat down for a talk, just man to man.

And in the last chapter I have poked into your family affairs . . . but here too with the benefit of professional counselors in family financial problems.

Our economy is full of wealth to give you solid security, even considerable luxury. There is no secret to the process. There is, to be sure, an element of chance, but you have seen how to make the laws of chance work somewhat your way.

You may make a million, ten million. I have seen many men, acting on similar principles, make much more money than I ever expect to see. More power to you! The drive, the integrity, the will to win must come from within yourself. But now you know the ways to encourage that drive and to take your steps in the right direction.

Index

Index

233